WHICH IS IT—
ONCE SAVED,
ALWAYS BORN-AGAIN?

CLARIFYING THE MISCONCEPTIONS
ABOUT CONDITIONAL AND
UNCONDITIONAL SALVATION

KOHNWAY PETER

WESTBOW
PRESS®
A DIVISION OF THOMAS NELSON
& ZONDERVAN

WestBow Press books may be ordered through booksellers or by contacting:

WestBow Press
A Division of Thomas Nelson & Zondervan
1663 Liberty Drive
Bloomington, IN 47403
www.westbowpress.com
844-714-3454

Scripture quotations are from the Holy Bible, King James Version (Authorized Version). First published in 1611. Quoted from the KJV Classic Reference Bible, Copyright © 1983 by The Zondervan Corporation.

ISBN: 979-8-3850-0001-2 (sc)
ISBN: 979-8-3850-0002-9 (hc)
ISBN: 979-8-3850-0000-5 (e)

Library of Congress Control Number: 2023910304

Print information available on the last page.

WestBow Press rev. date: 05/31/2023

Is Salvation Conditional or Unconditional?

Is It OK for a Christian to Continue in Secret Sin?

What New Converts Need to Know

Contents

Introduction

The explanation for undertaking this huge task by picking up my pencil to write this spiritual awakening and awareness volume is to theoretically and mentally educate readers and to put to bed the continual, controversial misconceptions about being a born-again Christian.

Moreover, many contemporary Christians assume that, once people have accepted Jesus Christ as Lord and Savior, they are saved or born again forever regardless of their continuing their habitual sinful lives. This assumption is very misleading and wrong. The Bible says, "Therefore if any man be in Christ, he is a new creature: old things are passed away; behold, all things are become new" (2 Corinthians 5:17). Here, we see that when people accept Jesus as Lord and Savior, they are new. The past is forgotten, and everything becomes new.

For instance, if sinners come to Christ, they are now changed people who are told to sin no more. They must get rid of their love for fornication, an adulterous life, cheating, stealing, and so on, and they must also do away with things that cause them to sin and instead begin living their new lives, which are in Christ.

Beloved, please do not be misled by those who believe that it is okay to continue committing immorality after accepting Christ. It is a wrong doctrine.

The right doctrine says that, after accepting Jesus, we must yearn for more positive changes in our lives—for example, regeneration, renewal of the mind and heart, and a new life that is solely geared toward doing the will of God.

Furthermore, other believers think that when people have accepted Christ and have repented from all known transgressions, they are saved or born again. This is accurate, but their salvation and security are conditional.

These can be secured if the people continue living through faith in Jesus and in the spiritual path of obedience to the rule of God, being dead to sin, which means they have no appetite for transgression.

In our spiritual journey, we might mistakenly or unknowingly commit sin, but we must accept the responsibility and immediately repent, be remorseful for infringing, and ask for forgiveness. Such a process must be executed in a timely manner, and we must be sorrowful and regretful for our actions.

Additionally, some well-known and learned believers will argue, "If you're saved once, you are saved forever. Our continuation in sin does not matter; God does not count that against us." Can you imagine how others interpret the scripture about salvation? For instance, what about a sister in a church choir who is willfully fornicating with a brother playing the piano? Both members have accepted Jesus Christ as their Lord and Savior, and the church considers them born-again Christians. Though both individuals are devoted Christians, are they genuinely born-again believers?

Must these members continue to sin that grace may abound (Romans 6:1–2)? A person who longs to continue in immorality exhibits a misconception of His grace and contempt for Jesus's sacrifice.

It is imperative that we comprehend the truth about what the scripture says. "God hates sin!" no matter how others might try to make it sound. A follower of Jesus Christ who is in the habit of intentionally transgressing against the will of God is not saved or a born-again Christian.

Another scenario involves a brother inviting a sister to church and encouraging her to seek salvation. Astonishingly, she discloses to him a text from a pastor at a church she had been visiting, persuading her to commit adultery with him. This man of God is legally married with kids, and this sister is married with a family as well.

According to her story, she has been rejecting his advancements toward her and his promiscuity. "I have been praying and wishing for him to stop intimidating me, but he does not take no for an answer," she says.

I believe this pastor is a womanizer and has no understanding that the behavior in which he is indulging is an immoral act that is not healthy for him, his ministry, or his family. Is this man of God genuinely born again? Do you think his salvation is secured and unconditional?

I keep bringing this up for those who do not know or comprehend that

God does see every wrongdoing in us, inwardly and outwardly. There is no sin that we can hide from the Lord. So continuing to defile the house of God is done to one's detriment. But many think it's okay to continue to sin once they have accepted the Lord. They believe they are saved forever and that God does not see their sin anymore.

Stop deceiving yourself. It is not okay but an abomination! God is a God of order. A born-again Christian does not continue to consciously sin after coming to the saving knowledge of God.

Therefore, any promise keepers, workers, or Christians who deliberately and knowingly commit iniquities in the vineyard of God or even outside the church are not genuinely born-again Christians and not fit to meet Christ on His return. They must genuinely repent of all known sin and forsake it.

Unfortunately, most of these converts who have fallen victim to some unsaved promise keepers and workers in the vineyard of God are ashamed to expose their offenders. May the Lord God regenerate and renew our hearts and minds to sincerely repent of all known sins, surrender all to Jesus, and be genuinely born again, in Jesus's name!

Foreword

Pondering and following what I continue to hear from many modern-day believers who profess to be born-again Christians have made for numerous restless nights, a long journey, and a worrisome era in my life, especially because these people are still living in perpetual sin. Continuing to live in darkness without acknowledging that deception affects all of Christendom and is a complicated issue that requires effectual, fervent prayer and a wake-up call to help set our acts right.

Professing Christians with worldly lifestyles, pollute and corrupt (Hosea 9:9; Isaiah 1:4; Galatians 6:8; Genesis 6:12; Deuteronomy 31:29) the servants of God with godly intentions. They assume that they are born-again with the misconception of not comprehending, what it really means to be a born-again Christian.

I have met with many of these folks, and they consider themselves to be saved and sanctified followers of Christ. And yet they are still entirely dependent on earthly, temporal things.

According to 2 Corinthians 4:18, "While we look not at the things which are seen, but the things which are not seen: for the things which are seen are temporal; but the things which are not seen are eternal."

Despite these warnings, we are not hearing or slowing down to listen. The above-mentioned beloved people have no intention of reverting to the Lord.

Repentance is not what they want to do at this moment. Instead, they behave no differently than unbelievers. They conduct themselves in the same manner and with the same character. They walk the same walk, talk the same talk, and dance the same dance as unbelievers, and because of that it is difficult to distinguish true believers from unbelievers. Are we born-again Christians?

Moreover, according to the word of God in 2 Corinthians 6:14–17, "Be ye not unequally yoked together with unbelievers: for what fellowship hath righteousness with unrighteousness? And what communion hath light with darkness? And what concord hath Christ with Belial? Or what part had he that believeth with infidels? For ye are the temple of the living God; as God hath said, I will dwell in them, and walk in them; and I will be their God, and they shall be my people. Wherefore come out from among them, and be ye separate, saith the Lord, and touch not the unclean thing and I will receive you." Is the Holy Ghost dwelling in today's believers?

Every living soul is God's creation. We were separated from Him by our forerunners, and because God loves us so much, He sent His only Son, Jesus Christ, to come and die for our sins, take our place on the cross, be buried in the grave, and rise again after three days to sit on the right side of His Father.

Once you have heard the gospel salvation message and realized that you are a sinner and are convicted, confessed, and accepted Jesus Christ as Lord and Savior, you are saved and need not sin anymore. But if you continue sinning and pretend that you are a born-again Christian, you are deceiving yourself and those close to you. My beloved, continuing in this state of denial indicates to me that you are not a born-again Christian but a professing Christian with a worldly lifestyle.

If you find yourself fitting the description above, please repent (1 John 1:6–9) now! Do not wait another moment because there is no time on our side. The misconceptions and posturing that are ruining the lives of innocent, incoming souls are worrisome. I ponder, praying for God's mercy and supplicating for an antidote to awaken our spirits and focus on being genuinely saved Christians.

Nowadays, it is kind of disheartening when finding it complicated to differentiate among countless contemporary born-again Christians and those who are genuinely born again. I cannot tell the difference because many of us currently still find it difficult to completely forsake our old ways (2 Corinthians 5:17) and surrender (James 4:7) to God.

Many of us are consistently making the same mistakes and expecting different outcomes. Innumerable Christians are still practicing the same things we used to do before accepting Jesus Christ as our Lord and Savior.

The only way for us to be genuinely born again and become true servants of God is to show our sincere interest in hearing the good news of Jesus Christ and accept the gospel salvation message by receiving Christ into our hearts. We must repent, turn away from all known sins, and believe that Jesus Christ is the only Son of God, who took our place on the cross for the transgressions of humankind.

Occasionally, a person can be instantly born again or saved by the intervention of the power from above, such as Moses and Paul. Moreover, it is essential to recognize that changes do not come easily when we have not made up our minds to genuinely repent of all known sins. Sin in the life of a Christian is a continuous pandemic that negatively affects careless believers.

If we do not examine ourselves and daily walk with the Lord, ensuring that we are still on track, we might be on the verge of destruction along with unrepentant folks and experience separation from our savior. It is unbelievable and frustrating for many of us who have proclaimed to be born-again Christians and yet still fornicate, live an adulterous life, and worship idols (loving any human being or thing more than God).

Astonishingly, we continue to ponder whether it is okay to live a sinful life, full of darkness, while pretending and deceiving others. We will be surprised to discover that someone we go to church with is secretly living a double life. Furthermore, many workers in the house of God are defining their positions in the church of God as professional jobs while living contrary to what they teach.

There is a popular statement: "Brother, though I am a born-again Christian and leader in the church, I am a human being like anybody else." On many occasions, I have asked questions, out of curiosity, to comprehend their mindset. I had a privileged meeting with a brother who was struggling with a commitment issue. I asked him, "Do you think it is okay, after accepting Jesus Christ as Lord and Savior, to continue in iniquity?" He paused for a while and responded, "I am told we will keep on trying till we get it or get there."

I went on, encouraging him and reminding him of the expectation and hope I have in Jesus Christ. I shared with him that there is hope for everyone who is sincerely trying to do the right thing by turning away from all known sins, forsaking things that cause immorality, and following the Lord.

Our generation is privileged in our ability to access the gospel in a variety of ways and dimensions. Nowadays, the right salvation messages are available and accessible on multimedia platforms and through internet-based technology, including Facebook Live, YouTube, Zoom, and others. However, in some underdeveloped countries, people who are genuinely seeking salvation and yearning to accept our Lord and Savior Jesus Christ do not have the gospel or cannot afford to access it. Some of them are finding it challenging to take delight or pleasure in these privileges of which we in the West and other geographical areas are fond.

By the grace of God and with the ingenuity of biblical scholars and spiritually filled believers of our days, it is a possibility that every soul on earth will have the opportunity to hear the gospel of Jesus Christ and read the Pentateuch for themselves. Because people can experience spiritual transformation only when they hear the gospel's salvation message, it is essential that these internet devices be available and accessible in other parts of the world.

Also, for those who are just careless or feeling left out, there is a unique way for those who are willing. By just acknowledging that they are sinners and need a savior, they are on the right path to salvation.

As sinners, it is okay to lay aside pride, our proud spirits; honestly confess and feel remorse for our sins; and repent of all known iniquity. In this manner, we are on the way to doing the right thing that will eventually bring changes to our lives.

Beloved brethren, we all know that Jesus Christ first offered us His love (1 John 14:19). Because He loves us and wants us to find redemption from sin, is it okay to deceive ourselves as His servants and secretly continue to commit immorality in or outside of the church?

No! But there is a course of action that will assist us as people struggling with the issue of sin in repenting. We must be committed and remain in Him as truthful and trusted servants.

I have pondered this procedure, and I find that it is the best way of immediately realizing that you are a transgressor, guilty, tired of being disobedient, and needing a drastic and dramatic change or total turnaround.

It does not stop there, but it starts with confessing all transgressions, repenting from all known iniquities, and asking the Lord for forgiveness and mercy (1 John 1:9–10). He is faithful and just to forgive everyone their sins, and then they should sin no more. Once you have played your part, He will do the rest by taking your plea and supplication into consideration, forgiving you, and having mercy on you for taking that bold first step.

My dear beloved, accepting Christ as Lord and Savior means saying no to immoralities, no to friends who encouraged you to commit iniquity continuously in the past, and no to old habits that caused you to transgress against the Lord and putting a stop to relationships and things that you could not resist. Additionally, please be aware that you cannot be in Christ and still commit sin.

Now, you are a new person in Christ. At this pivotal point in your life, there are a couple of spiritual exercises you need to consider:

- You must first surrender yourself to experienced spiritual leaders and devoted, believing friends in your local church or assembly.
- Listen to their teaching and learn from the salvation messages.
- Study the scripture daily and meditate patiently on what you have learned.
- Ask questions on any scriptural materials or Bible verses you don't understand, and at the same time allow that transformation to take its course in your life.
- Trust in Jesus Christ, and you won't regret it.

Moreover, it does not matter how long people have been Christians; once they have not fully repented from all known sin, they are still sinners. What matters is a heart that is willing to hear the gospel and accept it.

The Bible says in Hosea 4:6, "My people are destroyed for lack of knowledge: because thou hast rejected knowledge, I will also reject thee, that thou shalt be no priest to me: seeing thou hast forgotten the law of thy God, I will also forget thy children."

The majority of the followers of Christ came with diverse intentions. Some came with accepting hearts and minds to remain obedient servants in the Lord's vineyard, while others came with divided hearts and minds filled with doubts and unbelief and constantly rising and falling from the faith.

Thus, as a born-again Christian, it is of paramount importance that you examine your spiritual strength, ability, tenacity, and relationships; repent of all known sin; be genuinely born again, sanctified with a pure heart; and live a holy and righteous life daily.

Remember, being a bona fide church member does not mean you are also a born-again believer. It takes willingness of the heart and mind and the desire to make such an impactful move and decision of this nature.

Realistically, it is not that easy for anyone to abandon the wondrous, enjoyable worldly lifestyle and totally accept the transformation that inspired those who believed enough to unfriend the world and its temporal enticements. In some instances, it takes a touch of the Holy Spirit.

Hence, flowing with the crowd of church folks does not make anyone a saved Christian. You must go through the same steps that all sinners are required to go through to be born again, except in instances of divine intervention of the Lord's choosing, like in the cases of Moses and Paul.

In Exodus 3:1 and 4:17, we see that Horeb, which is also well known as Mount Sinai, is the place where Moses encountered God (Yahweh or Jehovah). Exodus 3:2 says, "And the angel of the LORD appeared unto him in a flame of fire out of the midst of a bush, and he looked, and behold, the bush burned with fire, and the bush was not consumed." This biblical account indicates that the burning bush is the site at which Moses was chosen by Yahweh to lead the Israelites out of Egypt and into the promised land.

Also, as Saul neared Damascus on his voyage, a light from heaven unexpectedly flashed around him. Instantaneously, he fell to the ground and heard a voice saying to him, "Saul, Saul, why do you persecute me?" "Who are you, Lord?" Saul asked. "I am Jesus, whom you are persecuting," he responded. (Acts 9:1–9; 22:6–11; 26:9–20). On the highway to Damascus, Saul experienced a dramatic conversion that amazed everyone in his era.

Likewise, as a born-again Christian, let others see those transformations and conversions in you through your demeanor, habits, and taking up the cross daily. Your encounters with the children of God and others must speak spiritual volumes.

Conversely, a life of confidential and continuous immorality does not represent Christ. As followers of Jesus Christ, we must live exemplified lives. If we do the contrary, obviously, others will begin to wonder how servants in the Lord's vineyard could carry themselves in this manner. As born-again believers, our Christian lives, integrity, and character matter.

Daily carrying the cross and Christian living must align or match with that which we preach. Though there may be adversity, Christ is with us every step of the way, as is the Holy Spirit. Please remember that we are not alone in this race. For that reason, He went for us on the cross of Calvary.

Born-again Christians should have heard the good news of Christ, been convicted by what they have heard, invited Christ into their hearts, received Him as Lord and Savior, confessed, repented of any known sins, and completely turned to Jesus Christ for their salvation. Furthermore, because of the ramifications of that inner and outward transformation, they have become part of the family of God forever and ever. This was entirely orchestrated and made possible by the spirit of God that works in us.

Also, you may well perceive that, by nature, we are not members of the family of God, and we have no right to inherit everlasting life. We have transgressed against God, and for that reason, the Holy Bible articulates in Ephesians 4:18, "Having the understanding darkened, being alienated from the life of God through the ignorance that is in them because of the blindness of their heart."

From this passage, we see that we were separated from God due to the adamant toughening of our hearts. We may not consider ourselves as immoral people; however, in the eyes of God, even a little sin is enough to derail us and stop us from entering heaven.

Nevertheless, because of God's unwavering support and love for us, He sent His only son (Christ) to save us by drawing us intimately closer to Him and making us part of His family forever and ever! Jesus made this sacrifice by dying for our sins on the cross of Calvary. He also conquered death with His resurrection.

As a people, we were born into an earthly family, and nothing can ever change that. Nonetheless, when we realize that we are sinners, it is imperative that we invite Christ into our lives and present ourselves to Him as sinful and wretched people, allow Christ into our hearts, confess, repent of any known sins, and turn to them no more! Then we must be baptized physically and spiritually and receive the Holy Ghost.

From this rudimentary beginning, we are born again spiritually into a heavenly family, which is the family of God. The Holy Bible expresses to the followers of Christ in 1 Peter 1:23, "Being born again, not of corruptible seed, but of incorruptible, by the word of God, which lived and abided forever." We have been born again. However, this should not be the end to the process of having a relationship with Christ (Ephesians 5:8–11).

Preface

The creed of predestined unconditional security for all Christians is a fallacy that is not taught in the sacred scriptures, and many are misled and misguided into accepting this inaccurate assumption. A person can be a genuine born-again Christian only when that individual remains obedient in doing the will of the Lord. One must willingly receive salvation, sanctification, and consecration through Jesus Christ. Such a person who has been blessed with the grace and indwelling spiritual effectiveness of serving our Lord and Savior will be steadfast in holy and righteous living through Jesus Christ, obeying the principles of God, and doing His will till Christ's second coming.

Unfortunately, many perceive such people to be deceived because they interpret the scriptures as saying, "Once born again, you are genuinely saved forever," regardless of the newly born-again individual's misconception, ignorance of the scriptures, and continued life of immorality.

Beloved! God hates sin. Anyone who is still willingly committing iniquities and at the same time serving as a promise keeper, worker, or church member is not genuinely saved and not born again.

The word of God admonishes us to not conform to this world but to be transformed by renewing our minds and hearts that we may prove what is good, acceptable, and perfect as the will of God. It is biblically and spiritually obvious and beyond all reasonable doubt that God is willing that all those believers should be saved (1 Timothy 2:24; Ephesians 2:8; Matthew 24:13; Romans 10:9).

Prodigiously and amazingly, untold numbers of people within Christendom past and present have been anticipating and professing that the Lord God's plan for us is that we must be born again. Being born again brings rise to new births, life, regenerations, and renewed minds, as well as hearts, through faith in Jesus Christ. According to the Bible, specifically in John 14:15–31, Jesus promises us the Holy Spirit if we love Him and keep His commandments.

Against this background, many might say that obeying His commandments is work and that, because He loves us so dearly, salvation was freely given. This interpretation misses the point, for salvation is unmerited. Christ shared His blood on the cross of Calvary for the forgiveness of our sins.

Let's be real here: Do you sincerely ponder whether, after inviting Christ into your life and accepting Him as your Lord and Savior, it is okay to continue living in darkness when He has sacrificed His life to set us free and reconcile humankind to God? Now, with the relentless assistance from the Holy Spirit, equipping us daily, there are some spiritual criteria that determinedly keep us faithful and in continual obedience in doing His will until Christ returns. Exceptionally, we receive these strengths through the inspiration of the power from above.

Blessed be the Lord God that Christians are privileged to have a heavenly Father who cares and is persistently watching over us. As His children, we must take advantage of the opportunity to live Christlike lives, which means living holy and righteous lives, till He comes.

The above-mentioned work of grace bestowed upon believers dynamically transforms our lives if only we are willing to genuinely repent of all known sins. Remarkably, the Holy Spirit works in us again and again! The degree of success depends on how willing we are to allow ourselves to be freely empowered by first, second, and third works of grace through Christ, which are salvation, sanctification, consecration, and so on. Obviously, these are generously given to us all! Why not make use of them?

When a follower of Christ is continuously experiencing being led by the Holy Spirit and seeing him- or herself full of the Holy Ghost, closely walking with the Lord God through obedience by faith in Christ, that individual is reassured of being a born-again Christian until Christ's Second Coming.

The major issues affecting all of Christendom are the problems of how securely the children of God can safeguard and happily preserve their salvation and sanctified and consecrated lives while they are occupied with worldly things, craving temporal roles, worldly lifestyles, and other things that pull them away from the Lord at every moment.

As a believer in and coworker with our Lord and Savior Jesus Christ, I admonish everyone to take a moment to meditate on how we can best make use of the works of grace, given to us through faith in Christ. Our foreparents were given choices to either genuinely serve the Lord God and be saved or to follow their own ways.

Today, our generation is faced with the same perception and options: either we steadfastly hear the gospel salvation messages, act by accepting Christ as Lord and savior, repent of known sins, and renew our minds and hearts or we continue deceiving ourselves and others until Christ arrives.

Can you imagine how it felt when it was too late for Judas Iscariot (Matthew 27:3–5) and Esau (Hebrews 12:13–17), just to name a couple? Judas regrettably realized the mischievousness of his conduct as a disciple in betraying Jesus, but it was too late. And out of disappointment and frustration, he committed suicide by hanging himself with a rope tied to a tree branch.

As for Esau, one day he returned home hungry from hunting and had caught nothing that day. Fortunately for him, his twin brother Jacob had cooked a morsel of delicious food. Esau asked for some, but Jacob asked him to first give his patrimony to his brother. Because he was very hungry, Esau complied and lost his birthright. As time passed, he understood the repercussions of his poor choice, but it was too late for him to undo it. The damage was done.

The scripture is detailed clearly for our learning, and therefore, it is important that we learn from people like Judas and Esau before our time on earth runs out. Remember that it is impossible for a dead person to repent from the grave.

Now is the time to repent (2 Corinthians 6:2b). At this moment, we have the great opportunity to yield to repentance before it's too late.

Beloved, it is essential for us to recognize that salvation through faith in Christ requires believers to be transformed spiritually. Sanctification purifies our hearts, and consecration separates us from things that cause iniquity and lack of dedication to serving Lord God.

Christians' lives can never be the same if they are genuinely converted through faith in Jesus Christ. The work of grace through Jesus enables our neighbors and other people to see Christ in us, and our deeply rooted purity positively changes our ways of meditating spiritually and how we approach, handle, and resolve issues. In that way, the follower of Christ is prepared and always ready to meet Jesus Christ when he comes for the second time.

But consciously and continuously showering in immoralities, disregarding the principles of the Lord God, deceiving those converts who are craving to know the truth, and expecting Christ to command and reward us for a job well done is foolish.

Moreover, it is spiritually imperative for the believer to continually practice the lesson taught in the Holy Bible about Christians' living holy and righteous lives. Holiness and righteousness exemplified in believers also prepares them and paves the way for living right before Lord God.

So, being a born-again Christian is predominantly what every disciple or anyone with the desire to follow Christ, must continue praying for while seeking the face of the Lord God until His Second Coming.

All these things can be accomplished only through faith in Christ. Also, it is critical that we make ourselves available to study the Holy Bible with understanding and find more time to serve the Lord God wholeheartedly. Remember that our salvation cannot be unconditional when we are continually disobeying the will of the Lord God and still enjoying immoralities and worldly lifestyles.

A person who lives in disobedience and transgression against the Lord God has a salvation that is conditional. No matter how we might sugarcoat it, what matters here is that living a Christlike life that will make us ready for the kingdom of heaven. Below are some spiritual tips we need to know:

- We must hear the right salvation gospel message with understanding and be eager to know more about what it says.
- God is holy; therefore, He is pure and hates sin. And anyone who comes to Him must repent of all known sin.
- I must admit that I am a sinner, and I must repent of all known immorality.
- A genuine born-again Christian does not sin.
- A child of the Lord God does not continue committing iniquities.

On the other hand, if for any reason believers are set up to commit sin or commit sin unknowingly, they should repent immediately and pray to the Lord God, expressing remorse for transgressing against His principles and promising not to repeat such an act. If we are faithful and sincerely bold in telling the truth and repenting of our sins, and turn to them no more, we might be kept on the right path with our heavenly Father.

Hebrews 3:4–6 says, "For it is impossible for those who were once enlightened, and have tasted of the heavenly gift, and were made partakers of the Holy Ghost, and have tasted the good word of God, and the power of the world to come, that if they shall fall away, to renew them again unto repentance; seeing they crucify to themselves the Son of God afresh, and put him to an open shame." Here, we see that Christians are secure as we continuously hold fast to the hope we have in Jesus Christ unto the end of time.

The gospel educates us that conditional security comes for all followers of Christ. Believers' final salvation, which is eternal contentment, is not automatic as many believe. It absolutely depends on you and me and an incessant conformity to the word of God. Followers of Christ are no longer safe if they backslide and return to the sinful lifestyles they once lived before turning to the Lord God.

Eventually, these individuals will be condemned with unrepentant sinners unless they repent and return to the Lord. Hebrews 10:38–39 says, "Now the just shall live by faith, but if any man draws back, my soul shall have no pleasure in him. But we are not of them who draw back unto perdition; but of them that believe to the saving of the soul."

Believers must not jeopardize themselves by giving up their loyalty, salvation, sanctification, consecration, and faithfulness during occurrences and manifestations of adversity, temptation, and persecution.

Only the followers of Christ who persevere to the end shall be saved. The Bible says in 2 Peter 3:17, "Ye therefore, beloved, seeing ye know these things before, beware lest ye also, being led away with the error of the wicked, fall from your own steadfastness."

Acknowledgments

This book would not have been possible without the grace of God, giving me the strength and being unwearyingly down to earth with the love of my life. (As the saying goes, "Behind every successful man is a strong woman.") I want to thank my beloved wife, Lucia, for her passion, thoughtfulness, and diligence as she remained standing with me through the rough, prolonged journey of all my yearning to tap into the saving knowledge of our Lord and Savior Jesus Christ. She is prayerfully my firm defense and support through faith in Jesus Christ. My love, never stop praying for me to succeed in any spirituality related projects on which I embark.

My wife is a virtuous woman who is loving, caring, full of life, full of positive surprises, and willing to go the extra mile to love me and do the little things that make her family feel happy and blessed. She keeps us, as a family, aware that our home was built on a Christian foundation, and for that reason, we must continue living in that Christian culture of loving God, His people, and ourselves and continue giving.

Also, I am not forgetting our two lovely sons. Unseen adversaries have continuously hindered and denied them of their God-given right to live as tranquilly and normally as other kids, but for no known reason, they have not given up on Daddy. Our children are apples of the Lord's eyes (Deuteronomy 32:10; Psalm 17:8). They are divinely protected, loved, and cared for, and by the grace of Lord God, we are always delighted and excited about life.

The adversaries, with their immoral eye monitoring spirit, have been falsely attacking Jesus Christ of Nazareth in us because greater is He that is in us than he that is in the world (1 John 4:4). As they are attacking me and my family, what they do not know is that Jesus Christ is in us. We are peculiar people in the sight of the Lord God (Deuteronomy 14:2; 1 Peter 2:9).

When any unknown altar is fighting us in the darkness, it is fighting the omnipotent God, and because of His supreme power, it will fail and destroy itself, in Jesus's name!

Beloved, the voyage to completing this book was not an easy one, but through profound faith by Jesus and the awesome blessings of our Lord, I gained the exact strength to continue and complete the entirety of this prose writing.

Chapter 1

WHAT DOES IT MEAN TO BE A BORN-AGAIN CHRISTIAN?

The term *born again* (2 Corinthians 5; Titus 3:5; 1 Peter 1:3; 1 John 2:29, 4:7) is one Christians use to describe the new birth, or the experience, that happens in people's souls when they acknowledge Jesus Christ as the Lord and Savior who came to earth, sacrificially died on the cross of Calvary for our sin, and freely gave His gift of salvation.

After being born again, people experience holiness and righteousness. In 1 Peter 1:3–4, we read, "Blessed be God and the Father of our Lord Jesus Christ, which, according to His abundant mercy, hath begotten us again unto a lively hope by the resurrection of Jesus Christ from the dead, to an inheritance incorruptible, and undefiled, and that fadeth away, reserved in heaven for you."

Moreover, the Holy Bible reveals that the wages of sin is death (Romans 6:23), but the gift of God is eternal life through Jesus Christ our Lord. We are born again not of corruptible seed (1 Peter 1:23) but incorruptible by the Word of God, which lives and abides forever. God is a spirit (John 4:24), and those who worship Him must worship in spirit and truth.

Also, born-again Christians are saved through faith in Jesus Christ and by being spiritually mature in their walk with the Lord. They do not look back to sin (2 Corinthians 5:17) but continue to live sanctified lives that are consecrated, dedicated, and devoted to serving the Savior intimately and doing God's will obediently until the return of Christ. Jesus said in John 3:7, "Marvel not that I said unto thee, ye must be born again."

Furthermore, a follower of Christ is one who has experienced a

1

distinctive, remarkable, and dramatic conversion through faith in Jesus Christ, particularly a member of a certain church group who stresses this experience. The manifestation recalls the scripture in the Gospel of John: "Except a man be born again, he cannot see God's kingdom."

Additionally, being a born-again Christian marks that time in the lives of believers when they are spiritually mature with unshakable and unwavering faithfulness in Jesus Christ. In such spiritual people, others can easily see Jesus, get convicted by their Christian lifestyle, and increase their love for God and His people. Believers in this unique spiritual category, which we refer to as born-again Christians, are usually led by the Holy Spirit in conducting and handling spiritual affairs with caution while serving in the vineyard of the Lord and in their private lives.

They are individuals with spiritual integrity, godly character, and very careful and spiritual compassion who ensure the preparation of newly converted followers of Christ and teach them the way so that they will not depart from what they are learning.

They must exhibit exemplary and admirable teachings and live what they preach while remaining selflessly dependent upon the Lord wholeheartedly, meditating daily on the word of God, and doing His will. They are sanctified, consecrated, and devoted to the purpose of propagating the gospel until the end of time. So the understanding about being born again is an endless daily walk with the Lord, perpetually living a holy and righteous life through unwavering faith while spiritually being strengthened by His grace until the end of life.

According to the Bible, Jesus Christ says, "I tell you the truth, no one can enter the kingdom of God unless he is born of water and the spirit. Flesh gives birth to flesh, but the spirit gives birth to spirit. You should not be surprised at my saying, 'you must be born again.'"

Likewise, people who are spiritually saved by realizing that they have been sinners, confessing and repenting from all known sins, and accepting Jesus Christ as Lord and Savior will see their lives transformed from darkness to light and will experience a renewal of the mind, sanctified with purity of heart, as they continue in their commitment to serve the Lord through faith in Jesus. These are born-again Christians.

To be born again reflects a willingness of the mind and heart, and it carries a longing for salvation through faith in Jesus Christ. It delivers us from the self or the flesh, and from peer pressure, and offers a thirst for the gospel's salvation messages that help one grow in faith.

Born Directly from Above

According to John 3:1–3 from the Holy Bible, which is the living Word of the Almighty, there was a Pharisee named Nicodemus who was a religious leader, a member of the Sanhedrin, and a Jewish councilman. Wary of being ridiculed by others while seeking guidance from our Lord, he went to Jesus Christ during the cool of the day, seeking answers to his burning issues that had confronted him at an event prior to the cool of the day.

Nicodemus said, "Rabbi, we know that you are a teacher who has come from God. For no man can do these miracles you are doing, expect God were with him." Jesus Christ responded and said unto him, "Verily, verily, I say unto you expect a man is born again he cannot see the kingdom of God."

Beloved, kindly take a second to positively ponder how confidently and boldly Jesus responded to Nicodemus's inquiry for the truth with a quick, powerful, and piercing declaration that must have felt like a two-edged sword shoved right into his heart (Hebrews 4:12). Perceive what Christ is saying in this surprising word to Nicodemus regarding new birth or regeneration.

Supernatural Renewal of the Mind

The spiritual renewal of the mind occurs when Christians are restored or something in them is made anew. According to biblical accounts, when our foreparents were created, they had a perfect relationship with their Creator. But when they disobeyed Him in the garden of Eden, the relationship was broken and could not be restored except through the blood of a sacrifice.

Eventually, God sent His only Son, Jesus Christ, to come and take the place of humankind by dying on the cross of Calvary and rising again to renew our relationship with the Creator (John 3:16). Prior to our coming to the saving knowledge or faith in Jesus Christ, we were dead in our iniquities (Ephesians 2:1; 2 Corinthians 5:17). But when we desire to follow Jesus, we die to immorality, and our broken relationship with our Creator is renewed (Romans 6:11; Colossians 2:13).

As believers, we ourselves are renewed as well. "He saved us through the washing of rebirth and renewal of the Holy Spirit" (Titus 3:5). Though the followers of Christ will not reach perfection until we are in heaven with our heavenly Father, the Holy Spirit immediately commences the work in lives that will be completed on that very day (Philippians 1:6). If we are still following Christ, renewal is a continual process (2 Corinthians 4:16). Believers are still prone to transgression against the Lord. It is advisable and imperative for renewal to become a constant exercise or practice as we seek to live Christlike lives.

On the other hand, believers are called to be set apart from the worldly culture surrounding us and to dwell in the world but not be partakers of the world (John 15:19; Ephesians 4:17–24). We are God's holy people (1 Peter 2:9) and must not embrace the values of the world around us. This is made possible by a renewing of the mind: "Do not conform to the pattern of this world but be transformed by the renewing of your mind. Then you will be able to test and approve what God's will is, his good, pleasing, and perfect will" (Romans 12:2).

Also, the renewing of our minds is made possible through daily studying or reading of the Holy Bible, which is the word of God, and meditating on the scriptures; it is through the word of God that we are sanctified (John 17:17). Believers have been given the mind of Jesus Christ (1 Corinthians 2:11–16) so we can see the things of the world as He sees them.

When we habitually focus our thoughts on Jesus Christ and "things above" (Colossians 3:1–2), our minds are aided in the process of renewal (Romans 8:5). The possibility of spiritual renewal of the mind is available only for followers of Christ. It could be the physical rest of our bodies to allow them to continue functioning at their best.

Another spiritual renewal of the mind or rest is salvation. Salvation, in a general sense, is likened to rest, as believers trust in Christ, not their own works (Hebrews 4:1–11).

Personal Relationship with Christ

Our Lord and Savior Jesus Christ calls us friends in the Holy Bible (John 15:15). A relationship with Christ is one of intimacy and security, of being totally known and totally accepted. To be frank, it is not a relationship of equals; however, He is fully God as well as fully man, and as such, Jesus remains Lord of heaven and earth.

Furthermore, Jesus uses His supremacy to usher believers into greater freedom, which is quite different from most concepts of authority. He wielded His power through complete humanity, thus inviting us into intimate fellowship with Him. It is a relationship where we can be loved completely, challenged to grow in our faith, and transformed into the exact people Christ created us to be.

Moreover, we were created to know God and have a close personal relationship with Him. Also, it should be self-evident that Jesus Christ is the center of Christian living. After all, there is no salvation in anyone else (Acts 4:12), and at the heart of the gospel is the clarion call to follow Jesus Christ, to become disciples (Luke 9:23).

To have a comprehensive relationship with Jesus Christ, we must make *ourselves* available to commit to having a close, intimate, and personal relationship with Him. Nevertheless, many are suffering from indecision, unsure about starting a cordial, intimate, personal relationship with the giver of life. However, it's very easy: receive Him into your life, accept Him as Lord and Savior, repent, convert, and be saved.

Moreover, born-again believers are commanded and wholeheartedly committed to begin teaching and preaching God's Word to people in their families and to win them to the Lord before reaching out to their neighborhoods, villages, towns, cities, community centers, and the world.

On the other hand, those diverse people are themselves responsible for hearing God's Word, receiving it, and continuously doing what His Word instructs. The omnipotent God tells people how they should listen to His word, to the gospel, and how to receive it, obey it, and continue to do His will for the rest of their lives.

The tremendous authority of Jesus alone can generate the conversion all believers must experience in their minds and hearts. Those followers of Christ, who would like to dwell with the Lord in His kingdom, must renew their minds and hearts, as well as their lives. Jesus Christ's power is the power to save, a power that delivers us from darkness and brings us into the kingdom of His dear son (Colossians 1:13).

People who are genuinely born again have been delivered from total darkness, are full of the Holy Spirit, and proceed to have an intimate relationship with the Lord Almighty. They move into a higher level of service and into a new and enthusiastic Christian life, leading to profuse spiritual lives. This point in their spiritual lives is an era of boldness in confessing experiences and the relationship between them and Almighty God.

Also, Jesus strongly emphasizes that we be born of water and the spirit or else we cannot enter the kingdom of God (John 3:3–5). The Lord Almighty clearly tells us in the pages of the Holy Bible that we cannot enter His kingdom unless we are completely born again (John 3:3). Consequently, the main purpose is to push us to be genuinely saved.

For instance, 1 Thessalonians 2:13 (KJV) says, "For this cause also than we thank God without ceasing, because, when ye received the word of God which ye heard of us, ye received it not as word of men, but as it is in truth, the word of God, which effectually worked also in you that believe."

Despite the extreme opposition from the people of Thessalonica, some people there wholeheartedly received the word of God. In the above passage, we see how grateful and happy the apostle Paul was, thanking God for them because they received the undiluted word, "accepting it not as the word of men, but was in truth, the word of God," which worked in those who believed.

It had to be the word of God that the Thessalonians received. They rejected the word of men. Respectfully, the Thessalonians were difficult to please, in terms of presenting God's word to them, but they were not impractical. They did not terminate every word that came out of the preacher's training. Once it was the undiluted word of God, they accepted it.

Moreover, their minds were renewed enough to accept the word of God, but they were narrow minded enough to reject what was only the word of men. Finally, they obeyed the word of God, and it worked in them.

In the case of the Bereans, the KJV says in Acts 17:11, "These were more noble than those in Thessalonica, in that they received the word with all readiness of mind, and searched the scriptures daily, whether those things were so." Two interesting, pivotal points stand out here: In Thessalonica, specific Jews opposed the word of God, even to the extent of following the apostle Paul to Berea to stir up trouble for him there. However, the Jews in Berea received the word of God with all readiness of mind. Sit back for a second and ponder this "readiness of mind."

Regarding the first converts, Acts 2:41 (KJV) says that, during the historical, biblical day in Jerusalem, the Day of Pentecost, three thousand individuals "gladly received the word of God and were baptized."

- They didn't have to be enticed or pushed into receiving the word of God. They were ready and eager to be taught.
- They were willing to be humble and lay aside distrust or preconceptions.
- They were watchful that what was established and promoted as the word of God was actually His word.
- They searched the scriptures daily and, at the same time, prayed for divine understanding of His word.
- They were willing to believe and obey what turned out to be the word of God.

Prevention of Sinning

After recognizing and considering ourselves to be sinners, we must stop sinning, confess all known sin, repent of any known sin in the past, and turn away from those things that entice us to sin. This will help transform our spiritual lives and give us the cause, through faith, to hate sin. For us to continue hating sin, the Holy Bible reminds us in 1 John 1:9 (KJV), "If we confess our sins, He is faithful and just to forgive us our sins and cleanse us from all unrighteousness." So we need to acknowledge that we are sinners before confessing our sins to the Lord. The Bible also mentions John the Baptist in Matthew 3:5–6 (KJV): "Then went out to him Jerusalem, and Judaea and all the region round about Jordan, and were baptized of him in Jordan, confessing their sins."

During the momentous day when Peter preached to the people in Jerusalem on the Day of Pentecost following the resurrection of Jesus, many of them were convicted by the Holy Spirit and asked Peter what they should do. His response is recorded in Acts 2:38 (KJV): "Then Peter said unto them, Repent, and be baptized every one of you in the name of Jesus Christ for the remission of sins, and ye shall receive the gift of the Holy Ghost."

Distinguishing Born-Again Christians from Other Religious Groups

The beliefs of people who declare themselves born-again Christians are genuinely and straightforwardly distinct and unlike those of most other believers. The distinction is that they accentuate what Jesus recommends that His followers do, which is a baptism into water and the Holy Ghost and acknowledgment of the Holy Spirit.

By receiving divine power from above and being perpetually and permanently embedded with the Holy Spirit, we can be reassured that we will walk on those streets of gold and dwell in those many mansions in the place He promised to prepare for us to live with Him eternally in heaven (John 14:2–3).

As we dig deeper into this controversial biblical subject matter— and an undiluted clarity assists us in comprehending where we stand as believers—below are five points that give exceptional clarification on the differences between born-again Christians and people of other religious groups:

- We must understand the derivation of the term *born again*. It implies "born from above." It refers to a spiritual conversion that happens upon acknowledgment of Jesus Christ.

  Moreover, our Lord and Savior, Jesus, said to Nicodemus, "I tell you the truth, no one can see the kingdom of God unless he is born again" (John 3:3–7 KJV)." Many ecclesiastics recognize this as occurring when people choose to become children of God.
- Christianity includes the Holy Trinity, which means the unity of Father, Son, and Holy Spirit as the Godhead. That is, born-again Christians believe in one God that is divided into three persons: God the Father, the Son, and the Holy Spirit. Thus, fundamentally

speaking, Jesus Christ Himself is God. We steadfastly believe Christ was born of a virgin, died on the cross of Calvary, and resurrected after three days in the grave.

Furthermore, Matthew 28:19 is the Great Commission: "God ye therefore, and teach all nations, baptizing them in the name of the Father, and the Son, and of the Holy Ghost." Also, the virgin birth is implied in the Old Testament as early as Genesis 3:15, which promised that "the seed of women" would be victor over Satan and sin. It is also predicted in Isaiah 7:14: "Behold, a virgin will be with a child and bear a son, and she will call His name Emmanuel." Matthew 1:22–230 says, "Now all this was done, that it might be fulfilled which was spoken of the Lord by the prophet saying, 'Behold, a virgin shall be with a child, and shall bring forth a son, and they shall call his name Emmanuel, which being interpreted is, God with us.'" Luke 1:27 adds, "To a virgin exposed to a man whose name was Joseph, of the house of David; and the virgin's name was Mary.'"

- We are saved by faith through Jesus Christ. Obviously, born-again Christians believe that people are saved by faith through Christ alone, not by anyone's efforts or good works. When people proclaim "Jesus is Lord," confess all known sins, repent, and consistently continue serving the Lord, doing His will, they are saved from the Lord's judgment and will dwell with Him in heaven for eternity. We believe this salvation became possible upon Christ's death. He became a perfect sacrifice, as He had never committed any sin.
- Born-again Christians also believe in the resurrection power of the Almighty. Our faith is based on a living God since Jesus Christ was raised from the dead. It is said that this is how Christianity contrasts with other religions, as other religious leaders have died and remain dead.
- The ritual of baptism is used to symbolically identify with being buried with Christ and being resurrected or raised with Him into a converted existence. Nevertheless, born-again Christians explain that physical baptism must be preceded by a spiritual one, where an individual is taken out of the demonic realm and baptized into Jesus by the Holy Spirit Himself.

Chapter 2

HOW DO PEOPLE BECOME BORN-AGAIN CHRISTIANS?

People can become born-again Christians when they hear the gospel salvation message, acknowledge or admit that they are sinners, and understand that they cannot live up to the perfect standard of God by their own strength or efforts. Then they must request forgiveness for their sins, turn away from them, repent, and accept Jesus Christ as their Lord and Savior.

Moreover, the way in which we become born-again Christians is by instantaneous authority of Jesus Christ, unaccompanied by any person's endeavor to bring about that transformation. Only the awesome power of Jesus can generate conversion in the minds and hearts of people, and all who come to Christ must experience the new birth to participate with Him in God's kingdom of heaven.

The scripture makes it emphatically clear that "Except a man be born again, he cannot see the God's kingdom" (John 3:3). Consequently, we must sincerely serve and live a sanctified life that encourages every believer to live a life that is set apart, reserved to give glory to God, by spending the time we have on earth as holy (Romans 12:2; 1 Thessalonians 4:1–5; 2 Corinthians 7:1; 1 Timothy 4:12) and righteous (Matthew 5:10, 6:33; Psalm 34:19; Proverbs 11:30; 1 John 1:29). In the end we will reign with Him in the kingdom of heaven (John 14:1; Revelation 5:10; Revelation 20:4–6). Also, it is imperative that we dissuade pride, transgression, and disobedience and allow the Lord to us for His purpose.

Additionally, we must be born of the Holy Spirit. That will lead to spiritual farsightedness and alertness. It will renew our minds, sterilize our hearts, and provide us a brand-new power for understanding His will, as He plans for our new lives and for loving God and others. It will also provide us preparedness and conformity to all His obligations.

To become a born-again Christian, you will begin to experience an unusual spiritual sense of freedom from oppression and depression imposed by the enemy, which is the devil, and eventually receive peace and joy in your soul. Romans 5:1 says, "Therefore being justified by faith, we have peace with God through our Lord and savior Jesus Christ."

Besides, when we as Christians are at peace with ourselves, the almighty God, and our fellow people, we are spiritually strengthened, cannot be easily moved by peer pressure or worldly enticement, and cannot be made woeful. Instead, we will be joyfully and spiritually filled and not exhibit any of the works of the flesh (Galatians 5:19–21), including "fornication, adultery, lasciviousness, uncleanness, witchcraft, idolatry, hatred, variance, emulations, wrath, strife, seditions, heresies, envying, murders, drunkenness, reveling."

Galatians 5:22–23 says we "nevertheless will exhibit the fruits of the Holy Spirit, which include love, joy, peace, longsuffering, gentleness, goodness, faith meekness, temperance." And Romans 3:23 (KJV) says, "For all have sinned and come short of the glory of God. We acknowledge, we are all sinners and that the punishment for our sins is death. Because of our involvement in committing sin, we are unfit and unqualified to comprehend and experience the love God has for us, and because of this we are separated from the Lord spiritually." Romans 5:8 says, "But God commended His love toward us, in that while we were yet sinners, Christ died for us."

In the passage, we see that our omnipotent God, who loves us so much that He wants to restore us, transform us, cure our circumstances, and let us benefit from His love bestowed upon us, sent His only Son to die on the cross of Calvary for our sins, taking our spot and punishment. In 1 Corinthians 15:5–6, the KJV Bible says, "And that he was seen of Cephas, then of the twelve: after that, he was seen above five hundred brethren at once; of whom the greater part remains unto present, but some are falling asleep."

After Christ died on the cross of Calvary, He rose from the dead. John

14:6 (KJV) says, "And this he said to prove him: for he himself knew what he would do." Here, we perceive that Jesus Christ is the perfect and only way to the omnipotent God, and He provides us the gift of salvation. Ephesians 2:8–9 (KJV) says, "For by the grace are ye saved through faith; and that not of yourselves: it is the gift of God: not of works, lest any man should boast."

According to the scripture, the spiritual gift that is freely given to us by the Almighty God and that we receive through faith allows us to experience new birth (John 3:1–8). Accepting Christ as our Lord and Savior simply means wholeheartedly trusting in Him to come and dwell in our lives, take away our sins, use us for what He wants us to become while we continue fearing God.

Steps to Becoming a Born-Again Christian

We should commence our brand-new lives with Jesus Christ in a way that we can intimately interact with Him and have eternal peace through a relationship with our Lord and Savior. Sincerely begin to put into practice the following few steps:

- Understand the intent of God for your life. God's intention for us is peace, and He would appreciate our experiencing this joyous peace and everlasting life. In Romans 5:1, the scripture adds, "Therefore being justified by faith, we have peace with God through our Lord Jesus Christ." We are reminded again in John 3:16, "For God so love the world, that he gave his only begotten Son, that whosoever believes in him shall not perish, but have everlasting life." Likewise, we cannot forget John 10:10, when Christ said, "The thief cometh not, but to steal, and to kill, and to destroy; I am come that they might have life, and that they might have it abundantly."
- Learn the misconceptions and issues that cause us to not experience His plan for humankind and our separation from God. During creation, we see that God created man in His own image. He gave us free will and liberty of options, which accorded us the opportunity to either choose to live our lives according to His will

or to transgress against His principles, and this act of disobedience led us to separation from our Maker.

In Romans 3:23, the scripture says, "For all have sinned and come short of the glory of God." Romans 6:23 says, "For the wadges of sin is death; but the gift of God is eternal life through Jesus Christ our Lord."

Proverbs 14:12 states, "There is a way which seemth right unto a man, but the end thereof are the ways of death." And Isaiah 59:2 says, "But your iniquities have separated between you and your God, and your sins have hidden His face from you, that He will not hear."

- Acknowledge that Christ's sacrificial death on the cross of Calvary reconciled us with God. The Lord came to earth in the form of a man and died on the cross of Calvary for our sins. He was buried and rose from the grave after three days. He paid the penalty for our transgressions and reconciled us with God.

  In 1 Timothy 2:5, we read, "For there is one God, and one mediator between God and man, the man Christ Jesus." Also, 1 Peter 3:18 says, "For Christ also hath once suffered for sins, the just for the unjust, that he might bring us to God, being put to death in the flesh, but quickened by the spirit."

- We must receive Christ. It is of paramount importance that we believe in and accept Jesus Christ as our Lord and Redeemer.

John 1:12 says, "But as many as received him, to them gave he power to become the sons of God, even to them that believe on his name." Romans 10:9 reads, "That if thou shall confess with thy mouth the Lord Jesus and shall believe in thine heart that God hath raised him from the dead, thou shalt be saved."

Thus, to accept Jesus Christ into your heart and life, do the following:

- Be remorseful for your sins and admit that you are a sinner.
- Repent of all known sins and sin no more.
- Accept your salvation through faith in Jesus Christ.

- Believe that He is the true son of God, who came in the form of a man, died for you on the cross, rose from the grave, and ascended to heaven.
- Accept Him as Lord and Savior through prayer, meditating on the gospel, and allowing Him to take control of your life through the Holy Spirit.

What Do We Look for in a Born-Again Christian?

When we become genuine born-again Christians, we will begin to perceive major transformations in our lives that are peculiar and that we are unable to interpret in the natural mind. Then, when we apply our own efforts to achieving these changes in our lives and in who we are, we become more spiritually awake, bold, and jollier Christians.

To be authentic born-again Christians, we must first hear the gospel's salvation message and believe in the good news of Jesus Christ. At this point in our spiritual lives, we must read and study the Holy Bible daily, pray effectually, and seek the face of God until He finds it expedient to give us new minds and hearts. We must yearn for it and hope for it.

The scripture also mentions that we are born again by the incorruptible seed, which is the word of God, and the gospel preached to us (1 Peter 1:22–25). So when people are born physically, they are children in their households. But when they are born again spiritually, they become spiritual children of the omnipotent God and an affiliate of God's household. This instantaneous procedure is parallel to the birth of livestock or to the reproduction of a plant. Hence, birth is the product of a seed that is planted, germinates, and produces a new organism.

Speaking of spiritual seed, the seed in question here is God's word, through which you and I become the children of God (Luke 8:11). God's word is planted in our hearts and minds when we hear the good news. James 1:18 and 1 Corinthians 4:15 say that, as we hear the message, believe, and obey it, we become born-again Christians.

On the other hand, if we erroneously plant the wrong seed in our gardens, we will not germinate the plant we expected to grow. And if we receive corruptible seed or a spiritual message that is contrary to the undiluted and true gospel of Jesus Christ, we will not truly be born-again Christians. Although we might believe that we have been born again, in spiritual actuality, we have not. We might just be consistent bench warmers in the church of the living God, our Maker, and not truly be born-again Christians.

So we must check ourselves by observing fathers and mothers in the Lord, the way Jesus has reiterated to us to live our lives, as we follow in His footsteps and His will and daily use our spiritual lives as examples to ensure that we have repented and totally surrendered!

You Must Believe in the Word of God

To have the power or right to become God's child, you must believe in Jesus as your Lord and Savior and as the only son of God, who came and died for us, says John 1:12.

For instance, let's say you have purchased a ticket to a Phillies baseball game, but unfortunately, a few hours before the game starts, a torrential rain begins. The weather turns out to be unpromising, so you don't go to the game. The ticket gave you the right to enter the arena, but it did not automatically make you involved. Other things had to occur subsequently. That is how we must use our new hearts to listen to the Almighty God, to walk in the spirit, and to be baptized with water.

In another example, let's say you frequently receive letters from financial institutions saying that you have been approved for a credit card or a loan. The approval gives you the power to get a credit card, but that does not mean you automatically have the card in your possession. Additional things must occur for you to receive the card.

In the same way, exercising faith gives you the power to become God's child, but it by itself does not immediately make you God's child. Other things must occur subsequently.

You can be born again only by rebirth, by renewing your mind, and by doing the will of God and not the will of man, says John 1:13. Remember that the word of God is the seed that makes us children of God. Additional seeds, such as manufactured doctrines, do not have the power to save. So it follows that the only way you can know that you are born again is by knowing what the word of God says about it.

Biologically Born Again

Ephesians 2:8–9 expresses, "For it is by grace you have been saved, through faith—and it is not of yourselves, it is the gift of God—not by works, consequently that no one can boast." When people are saved, they have been born again, are spiritually renewed of the mind, and are now children of God by the right of new birth. Trust in the Lord, in the One who sacrificed His life and paid the penalty for our sins. Because He died on the cross of Calvary, we can be born again. "Hence, if anyone is in Christ, he is a brand-new creation: the old self has gone, the new the new has come!" (2 Corinthians 5:17).

A born-again Christian is a new birth of a Christian or a spiritual renewal of the mind of a Christian, not a physical birth. It is a completely spiritual mindset that turns away from a sinful life to a genuine relationship with our Lord and Savior Jesus Christ.

In our pilgrim journey, while serving the Lord, some of us realize that the momentum we initially had when we acknowledged Christ has turned cold (Matthew 24:12–13; 2 Timothy 3:1–5 KJV), and eventually, we return to our former sinful lives. At this point, we are just Christians warming churches' pews, not actually born-again Christians.

For Christians who are born again, life is transformed from an old, unruly one to an excellent and obedient way of life through faith in Christ! And now is the time for a new beginning and an abundant life available for the purpose of Jesus Christ. We make ourselves available for Him to use us as instruments that we may work for Him.

Basically, this is the time to take baby steps in the right direction by walking intimately with the Lord. We must surrender all negative thoughts, doubts, and ideologies and be dependent on Him for everything. Also, we must be eager in seeking His perfect will for our lives and doing His will daily.

Avoid All Known Sins

Sin has been embedded into humanity since our ancestor Adam broke God's law in the Garden of Eden. Adam was directed by Almighty God to eat of all trees in the Garden of Eden when he was a caretaker but was warned to not touch or eat from the tree of life (Genesis 2:17b, 3:3b).

Despite the warning, Adam went ahead and ate from the tree of life anyway. Because he did not adhere to God's ordinance, he was driven out of the garden.

According to the scripture in Genesis 3:24, when the omnipotent God visited Adam in the Garden of Eden during the cool of the evening, Adam realized that he and his wife, Eve, were uncovered (naked), and they were ashamed to appear before the Lord Almighty God.

God, being a merciful savior, gave them fig leaves (Genesis 3:1–21, 24) to cover themselves and drove them out of the garden. Meanwhile, any child born of man is a sinner; we all inherited that from Adam and Eve.

Adam's inability to obey the principles and perfect will of God brought condemnation upon humankind, and we have been the partakers of it since Adam and Eve were driven from the Garden of Eden.

We are partakers through inheritance. Adam and Eve were our forebears, and whatever they did in the past, from the inception and creation of humanity, still affects us. Consequently, we must accept Jesus Christ as our Lord and Savior, believing wholeheartedly that Christ is the only son of God, who was born of the Virgin Mary, lived among us, was crucified on the cross of Calvary, died, was buried, and after three days in the grave, rose again from the dead and ascended (Luke 24:50; Acts 1:9–12) to heaven.

Chapter 3

WHO IS A BORN-AGAIN CHRISTIAN?

A born-again Christian is a person who has a personal, genuine relationship with our Lord and Savior Jesus Christ. Born-again Christians believe that Jesus Christ is the only Son of God, who came to earth in the form of a man and purposely died for our sins to set us free by taking our place and reconciling us with God.

These people have recognized that they are sinners, have been convicted, have confessed their sin, and have seen that their conversion has helped transform their lives from darkness to light through faith in Christ. Also, their transformation has led them to forsake all known wrongdoing, and the ramifications have led them to renewed minds and hearts and to pure and sanctified lives.

Being a Christian is intimately associated with the concept of an effectual call of God's spirit, which ushers sinners into an intimate relationship with Him through faith. According to the apostle Paul, "God is faithful, by whom ye were called unto the fellowship of His son (1 Corinthians 1:9).

Moreover, regeneration is the inward working of the spirit that induces sinners to respond to the effectual call of our Lord and Savior. The work of the Holy Spirit—convincing sinners of their sinfulness and misery and enlightening their hearts and minds with the knowledge of Jesus Christ—is an effectual call.

According to the New Testament, the term *born again* is derived from an event at which Jesus Christ was present and participated in during His time on earth. When Jesus's spoken words were not understood by a prominent Jewish Pharisee named Nicodemus, he went to Jesus privately and asked Him for clarification on the term *born again*.

Jesus answered, "Verily, verily, I say unto thee, except a man be born of water and of the Spirit, he cannot enter into the kingdom of God." Nicodemus asked Him, "How can a man be born when he is old? Surely, truly they cannot enter a second time into their mother's womb to be born again!" Jesus responded, "Very truly I tell you, no human being can enter the kingdom of God except that individual is born of water and the spirit" (John 3:3–5).

Here, we can see the supremacy of Jesus Christ of Nazareth in that, unaccompanied by anyone, He is able to single-handedly do the transformation work in the mind and heart of a person who is willing to receive Him. Also, it is incumbent upon the individual whose heart and mind are prepared to experience the impact of the Holy Spirit and participate with the Lord in the brand-new life in the kingdom of heaven.

Likewise, born-again Christians have been delivered from darkness and immorality, enter an intimate relationship with the Lord, and have enthusiastic lives. They experience new births, a renewal of their minds and hearts, accept Jesus Christ as Lord and Savior, confess their sins, repent of all known sins, are delivered from darkness, and gain salvation, along with sanctification, consecration, commission, and life transformation devoted to serving in the vineyard of the Lord.

In addition, born-again Christians are spiritually filled and have love for Jesus Christ and God's people. They must have a love for people, be prayerful, and read the Bible daily with comprehension. Being born again and remaining born again until Christ comes are what matters and are intimately associated with the concept of an effectual call of God's spirit, which ushers sinners into an intimate relationship with Him by faith. According to the apostle Paul, "God is faithful, by whom ye were called unto the fellowship of His son" (1 Corinthians 1:9).

The Supremacy of Christ

Unaccompanied by anybody, Jesus single-handedly did the transformation work in our minds and hearts that everyone who participates with the Lord in the brand-new life in the kingdom of heaven must experience.

The term *born-again Christian* has been debatable and controversial and often raises misconceptions among the followers of Jesus Christ. Glancing at it from the inventive reference, we perceive that the meaning is not about physical birth, as many misinformed Christians may think, but about receiving from the Lord a spiritual renewal of the mind.

Meanwhile, the sin committed by our forefather Adam, which is referred to as the original sin and took place many centuries ago in the Garden of Eden (Genesis 3), resulted in all of humankind's inheriting a corruptible legacy because we were born into a corrupt state.

Now, for this purpose, human souls require being born again and made holy, pure, and righteous, just the way He previously created us. After the creation of humankind, our Creator gave us the free will to choose to serve Him. On the contrary, we can choose not to serve Him.

Personally, I am encouraging everyone to choose to serve the Lord without holding back. There is a great reward for everybody who hangs on, continues being obedient, and does His will to the end. He also gives us free will in making choices, in choosing right from wrong. Because of His endless love for us, He made available the scripture, which is the Holy Bible, for our instruction, correction, and guidance in the right way to live a better life here, now, and after.

Chapter 4

MUST AN INDIVIDUAL BE A BORN-AGAIN CHRISTIAN?

According to the Holy Bible, "Jesus Christ said, 'Verily, verily, I say unto thee, except a man be born of water and of the spirit, he cannot enter the kingdom of God. That which is born of the flesh is of the flesh: and that which is born of the spirit is spirit. Marvel not that I said unto thee. Ye must be born again'" (John 3:5–7). Any who have decided to follow Jesus Christ and carry the cross must have heard the gospel salvation message, received it, and accepted Jesus in their hearts, after which they must repent of all known sin and forsake it.

As a believer, you must be born again to prepare for the physical and spiritual challenge to come, as well as the second coming of our Lord and Savior Jesus Christ. You must be willing to give your life and career to be used for God's purpose, invite Jesus Christ into your heart, and accept Him as Lord and Savior. You must also believe that Jesus is the only Son of God, who came down to earth and died for our sin.

Believers must be born-again Christians to enter the kingdom of heaven. An instantaneous familiarity is worked into the lives of Christians who have received the renewal of the mind; become spiritually motivated; been delivered from the self, peer pressure, worldly enticements, and darkness; repented of any known sin; and turned to Jesus Christ for complete salvation.

Then they are able to rely on God, do His will, and routinely search the scriptures by reading the Holy Bible daily with clarity of mind. They must pray fervently and continue to serve the Lord wholeheartedly.

As a result of this new experience, believers become a component of God's family. At this pivotal point in life of experiencing this unique spiritual transformation, it is essential that believers tenaciously search the scripture and tirelessly pray for sanctification that will help them draw intimately close to our heavenly Father.

Remember what Jesus said in Luke 9:62: "And Jesus said unto him, no man, having put his hand to the plough, and looking back, is fit for the kingdom of God." This is the time for believers to be courageous in seeking the face of the Lord continuously, careful not to quell the indwelling spirit. Therefore, God's spirit works in us if we continue faithfully serving Him.

For instance, in John 3:1–23, Jesus participated in an event and plainly told the other participants who gathered at the time, "Except a man is born again, he cannot see God's kingdom." Nicodemus was confused. His curiosity led him to find out and to comprehend exactly what our Lord and Savior Jesus meant. With the fear of being ridiculed by onlookers, he privately went to Jesus during the cool of the day, and he got the answer to his questions. And Nicodemus's life was never the same.

Beloved, please be aware that the radical transformation of being born again is not based on your country of origin or your cultural background; it is a freely given gift of rebirth, personally offered by God, and not earned through our human merit or effort. We receive this gift by faith through the omnipotent God's mercy unaccompanied. Titus 3:5 (KJV) says, "Not by works of righteousness which we have done, but according to His mercy He saved us, by the washing of regeneration, and renewing of the Holy Ghost." Our Lord and personal savior saved us; we did not do it ourselves and it was not done because of our righteousness or anything we have done to deserve it. His mercy for us is unending.

Being a Born-Again Christian

Being born again or saved has been a controversial spiritual topic. The concept has been highly misinterpreted and led to misconceptions among the ecclesiastical leaders nowadays. It involves the transformation of the human heart, manifested in the believer by the Holy Spirit, which empowers the believer to comprehend and act upon the truth of the word of God.

According to John 3:3, Jesus manifestly told humankind that, "except a man is born again, he cannot see God's kingdom." To be born again is the rebirth or renewal of the mind. It is not a physical birth, like when a child is born, but a spiritual rebirth. This spiritual revival is received through faith from our Lord.

Many in the world's Christian population claim they are born-again Christians, but is everyone genuinely born-again? The term *born again* refers to people who have accepted Jesus Christ as their Lord and Savior, or liberator. Romans 3:23 says, "For all have sinned and come short of the glory of God." Born-again souls realize that they are sinners and that the punishment for their sin is death. Romans 6:23 says, "For the wages of sin is death; but the gift of God is eternal life through Jesus Christ." To cure our sinful condition, God sent His only Son to die on the cross of Calvary in our place—to take the punishment for us.

Jesus Christ, the only Son of the Almighty God, is absolutely the only biblical way to originate the regeneration and bestow the spiritual changes in the lives of individuals who are burdened with desires and have received the renewal of their hearts and minds. Our Lord and Savior Jesus Christ's supremacy alone can work the changes in the minds and hearts for all who would participate with the Lord in the new life in heaven. God's word is the one and only way to God. Therefore, the religion that comes from God is the only one that can lead you to God.

Chapter 5

WHAT MAKES A PERSON A BORN-AGAIN CHRISTIAN?

People who are genuinely born again have experienced salvation and sanctification, everything they have been taught has become factual, and they have developed a direct and personal relationship with the Almighty God. Born-again people are spiritually filled and have love for Jesus Christ and God's people. Such people must be people friendly and prayerful and must read the Bible and meditate on it daily.

Furthermore, being a born-again Christian is not something that happens just for a moment, a day, a week, a month, or a year. It is continuous, and remaining born again until Christ comes is intimately associated with the concept of the effectual call of the omnipotent God's spirit, which ushers the sinner into an intimate relationship with Him by faith.

According to the apostle Paul, "God is faithful, by whom ye were called unto the fellowship of His son" (1 Corinthians 1:9).

Chapter 6

HOW DOES ONE BECOME A BORN-AGAIN CHRISTIAN?

You become a born-again believer only through faith in the emancipating or redemptive power of our Lord and Savior, Jesus Christ, followed by genuine repentance, a willing participation in water baptism by immersion or rebirth, and Holy Ghost baptism. Also, the answer to this controversial and inimitable biblical question is "when the individual hears the gospel salvation message of Jesus Christ and acts upon it."

Let's prudently read the following scriptures, carefully selected from the Holy Bible.

> Not everyone that said unto me, Lord, Lord, shall enter the kingdom of heaven; but he that doeth the will of my Father which is in heaven. Many will say to me in that day, Lord, Lord, have we not prophesied in thy name? And in thy name have we not cast evils? And in thy name done many wonderful works? And then will I profess unto them, I never knew you: depart from me, ye that work iniquity. (Matthew 7:21–23)

> And hereby we know that we know Him if we keep His commandments. (1 John 2:3)

> Blessed are they that do His commandments, that they may have right to the tree of life and may enter in through the gates into the city. (Revelation 22:14)

Jesus Christ is unblemished, and He says that you must be born again to be qualified to see the kingdom of God. Taking the necessary steps, making the right decisions through hearing the good news of Jesus Christ, getting convicted, inviting Him into your life, and accepting Him as your Lord and Savior is the greatest decision you will ever make.

Now, after you have successfully gone through salvation and baptism classes and gotten baptized as He commanded, you have gained your salvation and are saved. But does the process of being born again end here, and are you proclaimed saved forever? No! You have just started the Christian journey and must make up your mind to continuously serve the Lord until the end of time.

Additionally, recollect that, after accepting Jesus into your life and believing that He is the only Son of God and that through Him you are saved, you must put away everything that causes you to be immoral and sin no more (2 Corinthians 5:17)! Contrary to the truth, and despite our precious new lives, some of us have the tendency to hide behind our title of "born-again Christian" and continue in secret transgression and disobedience. Are we still born again? Where is our first love, when we initially came to accept Him into our lives?

I realize that the response to the above question might not sit well with many of my brethren who do not comprehend or agree with the way I came up with my answer to this question. Some even claim it and vilify other Christians for this dispute, but that itself shows that these believers are not completely saved and have not really known the omnipotent God.

Many try to prove this by pushing the Bible and all the theology available. The alarming pivotal point of unawareness here is that we are deceiving ourselves and not God.

When people are born again, others will know and see Jesus in their lives. And their lives will be exemplified lives that will help others come to the saving knowledge of Jesus Christ.

We are saved not by our good works. But this is often up for debate, and this provides us an opportunity and a platform to search the scripture for ourselves and prove whether the answer given was wrong or right. Furthermore, it is disheartening to realize that most of us who proclaim that we are saved and born-again Christians are still not genuinely in the faith, because authentically, we are not even close to living and walking in obedience to God.

After being believers and followers of Jesus Christ for some time now, many of the greatest biblical scholars who ever lived—and none are exempted—arrive at a moment of passing on, as our forefathers and early believers did, for those of us who are still alive to have the privilege of allowing the Holy Spirit to help transform our spiritual lives. Many are still committing confidential transgressions against the Lord, but those of us who have come to the saving knowledge of Jesus Christ must continue sharing testimonies of how our lives were transformed to those who haven't heard them.

As a person longing to serve the Lord, you do not hear the gospel salvation messages and keep quiet. You must tell others about your encounter with the Lord. Now is the time to commit yourself to serving through faith, being obedient to the word of God, and doing His will if you are fortunate enough to still be here on earth until the rapture takes place (1 Thessalonians 4:17).

Where will we be when the trumpets sound (1 Thessalonians 4:), and through which gates will we enter (Matthew 7:14)? Will we go take the narrow path and gate that lead to life (Matthew 7:13), or will we burn in an everlasting hellfire of torment? The Almighty God loves us so much, and that is the reason He sent His only Son to take our place (John 3:16). How much more can He do to motivate humanity to live and walk in obedience to Him?

Moreover, saved Christians are those who have heard the good news, which is the gospel of our Lord and Savior Jesus Christ. They understand that they are sinners, confess their sins, repent of any known sins, and turn to Jesus for salvation. Because of that, they have become members of God's family forever and ever. All of this takes place as the Almighty God's spirit dwells and works in their lives.

Most importantly, by nature we are not part of the omnipotent God's family, and we have no right to inherit eternal life because of our immoralities. We have transgressed against and defied our heavenly Father. The Holy Bible articulates in Ephesians 4:18 (KJV) that we are not to be like unbelievers, "having the understanding darkened, being alienated from the life of God through the ignorance that is in them, because of the blindness of their heart." They are "separated from God's life, due to lack of knowledge, blindness, and the hardenings of our hearts."

Beloved, we constantly refuse to perceive ourselves as immoral people and believe that we are not bad, but in the eyes of God, even a single committed sin is enough to keep us out of the mansion our heavenly Father has prepared for us. Then, what will it profit us to gain the entire world and lose our souls? Our souls, the unseen beings, are spiritually essential to dwell in heaven with our Maker. All we must do is turn away (2 Corinthians 5:17) from secret iniquities and sin no more, begin searching in the scriptures daily, make ourselves available, join churches in our local communities, and give more time to attending Bible studies, revivals, and church services. We can also seek unique mentors in the church who can tutor us.

Countless Christians, some who have passed on, have been anticipating the return of our Lord and Savior Jesus Christ to earth. But is everyone spiritually prepared to meet Him? I honestly believe that those who are genuinely born-again Christians and are dedicated to consistently serving the Lord until He comes will be ready to meet the Lord.

On the other hand, Christians who continue to live in confidential transgression and immorality will be cut short. Now is the time to turn things around before it gets too late. Let us reexamine ourselves and our spiritual lives (Romans 10:8–13) to see where we have gone wrong and quickly rectify these mistakes for us to be right with Lord.

Are we believers ready to meet the Lord when 90 percent of Christians are still doing things of which they initially repented when they first accepted Jesus Christ as Lord and Savior? Many are still worldly while working, holding leadership positions, and even teaching in the church of God. Are you still a born-again Christian? Some are converting but lusting after things of the world.

And because of that, many are leaving the church of worship in uncountable numbers. I am not sure whether I need to enumerate names or list churches involved, but kindly check for yourself; visit neighboring worship centers that you used to visit decades ago. Are the people still there? Try to know fellow believers and look around your surroundings! What do you perceive, and what do you experience?

Once, I was told about a young, devoted, African male Christian who was in his late twenties and served as a Sunday school teacher. The entire church knew this brother as a genuine born-again Christian because of the way he conducted himself: humble, down to earth, dedicated to leadership, well-behaved, genuine, and respected by every member of the church. He was a dependable worker and devoted Sunday school teacher for about ten years. Even youths of the church came to him for spiritual counseling. Outwardly, the brethren perceived this young Sunday school teacher as the bright future of the church. What they didn't know was that he was confidentially committing sin within the congregation that would lead to his untimely death and, after he died, the secret of his transgressive behavior would be leaked. The secret transgressions by this spiritual and committed brother went on for several years without any members of the church being suspicious about it or noticing, but then, all of a sudden, this young teacher caught a protractive illness and passed on. When members of the church congregated at the cemetery to say goodbye and to bury the deceased, one of sisters in the church choir screamed. She burst into tears, and in a loud voice, she said to the crowd of mourners and worshippers, "Please stop! I have a confession to make. I have been committing fornication with the deceased. We have been having an affair for six unbroken years. I couldn't tell anybody because he told me not to disclose our affairs to anybody, and at times, he threatened me, saying that if I did tell anyone about what was going on between us, he would harm me. He even encouraged me to have two abortions because he didn't want any members of the church to know about us. He warned me to always keep our relationship secret." Everyone at the interment was shocked, in disbelief, and embarrassed.

Now, my question to you, my beloved, is, Was this Sunday school teacher truly a born-again Christian? As born-again Christians desiring permanent residence with our Lord and Savior in heaven, what lesson can we draw from this rebellious Sunday school teacher?

As followers of Jesus Christ, it is imperative that believing in Him as our Lord and Savior matters. As well, it is incumbent upon us that we thirst for purity of heart and clean hands (1 Timothy 3:1; Psalm 24:4), and living a double life in the church of God should not be our portion, in Jesus's name!

At times, it is worrisome to see many Christians who call themselves born again still living covetously in the house of God. Because of that, the true salvation message—a living and transforming word of God—is not heard in many churches, and countless churches wax cold (Matthew 24:12). And I presume that these people are just hurting and deceiving themselves (James 1:22; 1 John 1:8) by clearly denying the purpose for which we were made in the first place and the privileges we have on earth. Having one foot in a place of worship and one in the world will, in the end, deprive us from reaching the kingdom of God.

Claiming that you are a born-again Christian or a worker in the house of worship and a promise keeper while still being deeply involved in confidential fornication, adulterous living, and lusting after things of the world means that you are using the title to satisfy covetousness. Are you genuinely a born-again Christian?

Our Lord and Savior Jesus Christ came to take our place, save us from our sins, and make us a member of His family forever! He did all this for you and me by dying on the cross of Calvary and conquering demise through His resurrection.

Furthermore, as human beings, we were born into a household, and nothing can ever change that. However, when we hear the gospel salvation message and come unto Jesus Christ, we are spiritually rebirthed into another household, which is the family of the Almighty. In 1 Peter 1:23 (KJV), the Bible talks about "being born again, not of corruptible seed, but of incorruptible, by the word of God, which lived and abided forever." The Holy Bible articulates to followers of Christ, "We have been born again through the living and undiluted word of God."

Chapter 7

WHEN DOES A PERSON KNOW HE OR SHE IS BORN AGAIN?

When Nicodemus initially heard our Lord and Savior speak about being born again, he didn't comprehend what Christ meant. He was confused, imagining things in his head, just like others attending the event did. He didn't sweep the word that he heard under the carpet; he acted on it immediately by finding Jesus and asking Him to clarify what He meant by "born again."

Here, Jesus was given the opportunity and platform to preach the gospel salvation message one on one with Nicodemus. Likewise, Nicodemus was eager and willing to hear Jesus Christ interpret the meaning of how people must be born again. After Jesus carefully explained to Nicodemus what He meant, Nicodemus walked away joyously, a new man in a new birth and a born-again Christian (John 3:3–7 KJV).

Thus, a genuinely born-again Christian must base his or her faith on receiving our Lord and Savior by faith through the Holy Spirit for a more profound acceptance of Jesus Christ of Nazareth. Additionally, people are born again when they are chosen by our heavenly Father to be used for His purpose, which is instant divine intervention; when they hear the gospel salvation message being taught and are converted; or when they continuously hear the good news of Jesus Christ and accept Him as their Lord and Savior through faith.

Hebrews 4:12 (KJV) says, "For the word of God is quick, and powerful, and sharper than two-edged sword, piercing even to the dividing asunder of soul and spirit, and of the joints and marrow, and is a discerner of the thoughts and intents of the heart." As you listen to the teachings of the good news or the gospel salvation message of Jesus Christ, something unusual and inspirational rapidly begins occurring inwardly, dwelling in you because the more powerful, life-transforming salvation messages you hear, the more likely you are to receive the Holy Ghost through faith in Jesus Christ, which brings transformation into your life.

From the beginning or inception of your spiritual longing, you might not comprehend how it all works, but as you progress in your faith, you will start to understand that the awesome power of God is upon you. From this point on, you will experience spiritual awareness and see that you hate participating in the things that you used to enjoy (2 Corinthians 5:17). Instead, you will turn away from your sin to allow Christ to occupy your new life, which establishes indwelling spiritual and positive changes as you become more spiritually alert and as others begin to perceive those changes.

Equally so, your thirst (Psalm 42:1–2) and yearning for the God, our Creator, cannot be satisfied with precious stones or diamonds. Now is the time to focus on the things of God and to do His will.

In the phase you are reaching now, there is no looking back to participating in the things of the past. You will begin to perceive the bigger and greater spiritual experiences to come. Similarly, you will remain a born-again Christian if you genuinely continue to believe that Christ is your only Savior, serve Him faithfully daily, and live and walk in obedience to God.

From this pivotal point of being spiritually filled without wavering, being unshakable in times of persecution and demonic conspiracies, and being equipped with the breastplate of righteousness, continue living an appropriate, holy life until you eventually meet Jesus Christ. Only then can you have reassurance that you are forever saved.

Professing that you have accepted Christ as Lord and Savior does not mean you are born again and saved forever. You cannot consider yourself saved indefinitely if you are still secretly indulging in unscrupulous acts that cause you to continue sinning. That does not separate you from those who live disobedient and sinful lives.

Additionally, numerous past and present followers of Jesus Christ have communicated about having been born again. Thousands of evangelicals and tens of thousands of Protestants believe that, after becoming "followers of Christ," they have been born again. But what some of the followers fail to realize is what the phrase really means. They have heard the gospel and have been trained to understand that "confessing Christ" and accepting Him into their lives brings transformation. That is true. But to continue living a double life, in contradiction to a Christlike life, is unacceptable and might lead many followers to an unexpected end.

Believers, the goal should be to keep doing the will of the Lord until we meet with Him in heaven. We must live according to the standard He set for us and shine upon those who do not know Him. We must come unto the Lord through our Christian character, conduct, charity, integrity, and caring for others.

So, as a new convert and follower of Christ, you must begin to hate participating in things that cause sin. This includes avoiding evil communications (1 Corinthians 15:33–34) and yoking with an unbeliever (2 Corinthians 6:14).

From now on, you will experience hating to participate in things you used to enjoy (2 Corinthians 5:17), and you will turn away from your sin to allow Christ to occupy your new life, which means implementing changes and becoming more spiritually alert. Others will begin to perceive these changes. From this point on, when you thirst, you will not look back and partake in things of the past but strive to do all you can by the grace of God through faith in Jesus Christ to make it to heaven. According to the scriptures, there is a reward awaiting us in heaven.

Remember that a born-again crusade was widespread during a dissimilar era during the biblical centuries; nevertheless, the contemporary crusade had its start during the nineteenth century. Below are some evidential events that led to the rise of the born-again Christian crusade.

In John 3:3–7 (KJV), we read,

> Jesus answered and said unto him, Verily, verily, I say unto thee, except a man be born again, he cannot see the kingdom of God. Nicodemus said unto him, How can a man be born again when he is old? Can he enter the second time into his mother's womb, and be born? Jesus answered, Verily, very, I say unto thee, except a man be born of water and of the spirit, he cannot enter the

kingdom of God." He continued, "That which is born of the flesh is flesh, and that which is born of the spirit is spirit. Marvel not that I said I said unto thee, ye must be born again."

In this passage, we see that the rebirth of our Lord and personal savior Jesus Christ in person, when he participated in an event during His days on earth, can be traced to these scriptures. Nicodemus, a well-learned man, a Sanhedrin, and a Jewish leader, misunderstood what our Lord had said, and because he wanted to comprehend and was curious, he sought Jesus for clarification about "no one can see the kingdom of God unless he is born again." Jesus clarified to him by saying, "Flesh gives birth to flesh but the spirit gives birth to spirit. You should not be astonished at my saying you must be born again."

Chapter 8

WHAT IS SIN?

Sin is an iniquitous act deemed to be a contravention of divine principles and an offense or disobedience against God's rule. "Therefore, to him that knoweth to do good, doeth it not, to him is sin" (James 4:17). In other words, sin is a transgression against God.

Moreover, sin is a word spoken or unspoken, a thought, or an inappropriate action that differs from the divine principle or character of the omnipotent God. We all have sinned, according to Romans 3:23, and even what we consider charitable deeds are often tainted by egotistical motives or arrogance, as explained in Isaiah 64:6. We must see ourselves in the mirror, and it's left to us, although we know that it is absolutely impossible to please the Almighty God or to live entirely free from sin, as stated in Romans 3:10 and Ecclesiastes 7:10.

When folks come to Jesus Christ of Nazareth by faith, believing that He is the one and only Son of God, that He came and died for our sins, and that He was in the grave for three days and rose on the third day and ascended to heaven, as well as trusting Him to forgive and cleanse them of their sins, they are genuinely in the moment of becoming born-again Christians, says John 3:3.

That renewal of the mind and the rebirth by the Holy Ghost results in a new creation, says 2 Corinthians 5:17. The omnipotent God gives the repentant sinner or backslider a new heart that is turned toward pleasing and obeying Him rather than the self (2 Corinthians 5:9; Romans 8:5–6). Whereas we were in darkness and formerly slaves to sin, we are now being transformed and are slaves to righteousness (Romans 8:16). Sin's stronghold of controlling us has been broken to pieces by the awesome power of Jesus Christ (Romans 6:6; Titus 2:14).

Nevertheless, we as a people still reside and live in flesh. It is habitual and wants what it wants. According to Romans 7:21–23, the apostle Paul acknowledges the battle existing between flesh and the Holy Spirit in his personal life: "Therefore, I find then a law, that, when I would do good, evil is right there with me."

According to the Holy Bible, sin is transgression or breaking God's law (1 John 3:4). It is the act of betrayal against God's promises (Amos 1–2).

Are All Sins Equal to the Almighty God?

The Bible reveals that degrees of sin do exist. Some sins are more despicable to the omnipotent God than others. To prove this, let's read the following scriptures from the Holy Bible for clarity.

> For all do such things, and all that do unrighteous, are an abomination unto the Lord thy God. (Deuteronomy 25:16 KJV)

Six behaviors common to humankind are a disgrace to God; our heavenly Father does not like such behaviors. As believers, we are warned to not cross the line by indulging in such acts, which leads to detrimentally facing chastisement.

> And these six unworthy things the Lord hate, are abomination unto Him, which includes, a proud look, lying tongue, hands that shed innocent blood, heart that devised wicked imaginations, feet that is swift in running to mischief, false witness, lies, and he that soweth discord among brethren. (Proverbs 6:16–19 KJV)

Nonetheless, when it comes to the eternal consequences of sin, they are all the same. Romans 6:23 (KJV) says, "For the wages of sin is death; but the gift of God is eternal life through Jesus Christ our Lord." So, every sin, every act of rebellion, precedes condemnation and eternal death.

How Can Christians Deal with the Issue of Sin?

The outcries, misconceptions, and controversial matters affecting the lives of most believers and unbelievers in the past and present for the entirety of the Christian religion are all related to the issue of sin. As humanity has already established, sin is a consequential matter, destroying the sacrifice made by our Lord and Savior Jesus Christ.

Finding an antidote to this contagious pandemic, which many are having a joyous time reveling in daily while others are eradicating it from their lives to do the will of God, is that we must consistently continue sincerely seeking the face of God through tireless prayers and supplication for transformation.

We are privileged to have the following scriptures from the Holy Bible to undoubtedly clarify to us how deadly immorality is and how it can easily intrude into our lives when we are careless and complacent believers. Also, we will understand how consequential iniquity is and what the true color of sin is.

> But we are all as an unclean thing, and all our righteousness are filthy rages; and we all do fade as a leaf; and our iniquities, like the wind, have taken us away. (Isaiah 64:6 KJV)

> But glory, honor, and peace, to every man that worked well to the Jew first, and to the gentile: For there is no respect of persons with God. For as many as have sinned without law shall also perish without law: and as many as have sinned in the law shall be judged by the law; (Romans 2:10–12 KJV)

> Thou that makes they boast of the law, through breaking the law dishonors thou God. (Romans 2:23 KJV)

Beloved, if sin divides us from God and denounces us to death, then how can we be cleaned and free from the curse of sin? Mercifully, the omnipotent God freely gives us His one and only Son, Jesus Christ, as a lasting solution to our sin issues. Through Him, and by His sacrificial demonstration on the cross of Calvary, He solved the sin issue, and followers of Christ can seek salvation.

How Then Can Believers Judge Whether They Perceive the Appearance of Sin?

Uncountable sins are demonstrated clearly in the Holy Bible. For instance, the Ten Commandments provide us a full, undiluted, clear portrait of God's principles. These standards constitute fundamental regulations of behavior and integrity for spiritual and ethical living.

Countless other Bible verses exemplify direct instances of sin, and the scriptures provide general guidelines to assist believers in judging sin when they are not certain. Therefore, we need to be aware of iniquity and what we can do when we begin to experience sin creeping into our lives.

Typically, when we are confused about our uncertainty with sin, it is vital that we first search the scriptures thoroughly for answers. Second, we should examine our lives to identify any changes, asking whether something odd has occurred in the past days, months, or year.

Additionally, we must remember to align our contemplations and questions with the scriptures. Patiently following through with this straightforward process will absolutely assist us in acknowledging whether immorality is creeping into our lives or not.

Moreover, 1 Corinthians 10:23–24 (KJV) says, "All things are lawful for me, but all things are not expedient: all things are lawful for me, but all things edify not. Let no man seek his own, but every man another's wealth." So we must ask the following questions: Is there any good thing in this for me and others? Is this spiritually profitable and beneficial? Will it draw me intimately closer to the Almighty God? Finally, will it strengthen my faith in loving the omnipotent God and others and allow me to continue sharing the gospel as well as winning souls?

Furthermore, 1 Corinthians 6:19–20 (KJV) says, "What? Know ye not that your body is the temple of the Holy Ghost, which is in you which ye have of God, and ye are not your own? For ye are bought with a price: therefore, glorify God in your body, and in your spirit, which are God's."

From this passage, we can also ask further questions to help us understand and clear all doubt in our minds: Will this thing glorify the Almighty God? Will God bless what is coming into my life or what I am about to do and use it for His purpose? Will this thing be pleasing and honoring to the Highest God?

Similarly, Romans 14:21 (KJV) says, "It is good neither to eat flesh, nor to drink wine, nor any thing whereby thy brother stumbled, or is offended, or made weak." This may lead us to ask ourselves, *How will this concept affect me and my family, inner circle, and brethren?* Even though we have redemption in Jesus Christ, we are spiritually encouraged to certainly not let our redemptions cause a weaker brother or sister to stumble.

In addition, since the Holy Bible teaches us to submit to those in authority above us—for instance, parents, teachers, spouses—it is interesting to ask ourselves, *Do my parents have an issue with what I am doing or what I am about to accept in my life? Am I willing to submit this thing to those in leadership above me?*

Last, consider these verses: "And whatsoever ye do in word or deed, do all in the name of the Lord Jesus, giving thanks to God and the Father in him" (Colossians 3:17 KJV); "And he that doubted is condemned if he eates, because he eates not of faith: for whatsoever is not of faith is sin" (Romans 14:23 KJV). In everything, we are to allow our consciences to convict us before God of what is inappropriate and immoral on issues that are not clear in the Bible after we've read relevant scriptures. We must encourage ourselves and ask: *Do I have redemption in Jesus Christ and an unambiguous conscience before the Almighty to do whatever I am intending to do? Are my personal desires aligned with God's will in this matter?*

Then, What Should Our Attitude Toward Sin Be?

In Romans 3:23 (KJV), we read, "For all have sinned and come short of the glory of God," and 1 John 1:10 (KJV) says, "If we say that we have not sinned, we make Him a liar, and His word is not in us." The truth is that we have all sinned. The Holy Bible says this clearly, as we have read. But the scripture also expresses that the omnipotent God despises sin and urges us as believers to cease sinning.

43

Furthermore, 1 John 3:9 (KJV) says, "Whosoever is born of God doth not commit sin; for His seed remained in him: and he cannot sin, because he is born of the Almighty God." The Holy Bible is clearly warning us in the scripture that those who are born of God and are now considered family of our heavenly Father do not continue practicing immorality or living in sin, because the spirit of God and His life is in them. As Christians born of God, it is of paramount importance that we live holy and righteous lives, or Christlike lives that help us avoid practices that cause believers to sin. It is also imperative that we continuously meditate upon God's word. Whenever we are feeling weak, we must make it our duty to search the scriptures and pray for strength.

What, Then, Is Unforgivable Sin?

Mark 3:29 (KJV) says, "But he that shall blaspheme against the Holy Ghost hath never forgive but is in danger of eternal damnation." So if you habitually blaspheme against the Holy Ghost, you will never receive pardon but are in peril of everlasting perdition or eternal punishment. Matthew 12:31–32 (KJV) says, "Wherefore I say unto you, all manner of sin and blasphemy shall be forgiven unto man: but the blasphemy against the Holy Ghost shall not be forgiven unto man. And whosoever speak against the Son of man, it shall be forgiven him: but whosoever speak against the Holy Ghost, it shall be forgiven him, neither in the world, neither in the world to come." Luke 12:10 (KJV) adds, "And whosoever shall speak a word against the Son of man, it shall be forgiven him: but unto him, that blasphemed against the Holy Ghost it shall not be forgiven." This issue of unforgivable sin is one of the most difficult, challenging, and sensitive matters in walking with the Lord.

Types of Sin

Most believers are not aware of the other types of sin. They are iniquities that we commit every day without knowing it because they are common to humanity. We also have imputed sins, sins of omission and commission, mortal sins, and venial sins. These are briefly describes below.

Imputed sin

The book of Romans tells us, "Wherefore, as by one man sin entered the word, and death by sin; and so, death passed upon all men, for that all have sin. For until the law sin was in the world: but sin is not imputed when there is no law. Nevertheless, death reigned from Adam to Moses, even over them that had not sinned after similitude of Adam's transgression, who is the future of him that was to come.... Therefore, as by the offense of one judgment came upon all men to condemnation; even so by the righteousness of one the gift came upon all men onto justification of life" (Romans 5:12–14, 18 KJV).

Hence, when our forebear Adam sinned in the garden of Eden by eating fruit from the tree of knowledge of good and evil—which the omnipotent God had specifically warned him against—that act of disobedience generated dangerous consequence for all humankind. Imputed sin is one of two impacts that Adam's sinful existence had on humanity.

Original sin is the initial impact. As a consequence of Adam's sin, humanity entered the earth with a fallen nature. Also, the coverlet of Adam's sin is attributed to Adam and to every individual who came after him. This is imputed sin. On the other hand, humankind merits the same penalty as Adam. Imputed sin devastates humankind when standing before the Almighty God, whereas original sin devastates our personalities. Original and imputed sin put us under God's verdict.

Sins of Omission and Commission

Consider the following scriptures:

> Therefore, to him that know to do good, and doth it not, to him it is a sin. (James 4:17 KJV)

> And Jesus, answering, said, A certain man went down from Jerusalem to Jericho, and felt among thieves, which stripped him of his raiment, and wounded him, and departed, leaving him half dead. And by chance there came down a certain priest that way: and when he saw him, he passed by on the other side. And likewise, a Levite, looked at him,

and passed by the other side. But a certain Samaritan, as he journeyed, came where he was: and when he saw him, he had compassion on him. And went to him, and bound up his wounds, pouring in oil and wine, and set him on his own beast, and brought him to an inn, and took care of him. And on the marrow when he departed, he took out two pence, and gave them to the host, and said unto him, take care of him; and whatsoever thou spend more, when I come again, I will repay thee. Which now of these three, thinks thou, was neighbor unto him that fell among the thieves? And he said, he that shewed mercy on him. Then said Jesus unto him, Go, and do thou likewise. (Luke 10:30–37 KJV)

But whoso hath this world's good, and see that his brother has need, and shuttled up his bowels of compassion from him, how dwelleth the love of God in him? (1 John 3:17 KJV)

Let your light so shine before men, that they may see your good works, and glorify you Father which is in heaven. (Matthew 5:16 KJV)

And let not be weary in well doing; for in due season, we shall reap if we faint not. (Galatians 6:9 KJV)

And be not conformed to this world: but be ye transformed by the renewing of your mind, that ye may prove what is that good, and acceptable, and perfect, will of God. (Romans 12:2)

Moreover, preceding sins, which include those of omission and commission, pertain to personal sins. A sin of omission is committed when we disobey the word of God by not following what the scripture teaches; instead, we do the contrary. Such a sin occurs because of our not doing something that is right, failing to execute a command of God, or avoiding doing as instructed. For instance, we know fully well how to pray for others, but we neglect and do not intercede for anybody as well as we do with new converts, the oppressed, the sick, and others.

For example, suppose a pastor at a local church or assembly tells his congregation that they are not allowed to sing songs from a new hymnal, donated by a sister church, during their next meeting until all members of the congregation get a copy, but they go ahead and do it anyway. This a clear indication that the congregation has committed an act of disobedience. Another example is a pastor telling his congregation that every member should report to the church on Saturday morning to go out to win souls and none of them turn out. This is also an act of disobedience. Specifically, this is a sin not because of something they have done but because of what they haven't done.

As Christians, serving the Almighty God encompasses serving our families, friends, neighbors, and others. The more believers love the Lord, the deeper their hearts connect with His love. On the other hand, pride, complacency, and fear cause us to commit sins of omission.

A sin of commission or presumption involves willfully violating God's commands or being disobedient. It is a sin that we are familiar with and intentionally commit daily by transgressing against God's commands. It also includes the deliberate act of violating the omnipotent God's commands through our awful behaviors or by involving ourselves in something that we should have no part of, such as lying or stealing.

If a father cruelly beat his child unmercifully on a street corner for not doing his chores, every one of us would be enraged and repulsed. Or if a believer committed infidelity, every one of us would instantly recognize that that person has committed a sin. Such an act is identifiable as a sin of commission (presumption). As believers, we must involve ourselves when we see people doing things they should not do.

As we clearly comprehend and gain a deeper understanding of the sins of commission (presumption), the apostle Paul further clarifies in 1 Corinthians 6:10 (KJV), "Nor thieves, nor covetous, nor drunkards, nor revilers, nor extortioners, shall inherit the kingdom of God."

Venial Sin

Venial sins are believed by some denominations, including Catholics, to be relatively slight or committed without full reflection or consent. They are forgivable sins. Such sins involve acting as we should not without putting us into actual incompatibility with the state of grace that mortal sin implies. They do not break a person's relationship with God but injure it. Venial sins are contrasted with mortal sins.

Although a venial sin is obviously a sin that weakens the sinner's union with God, it is not a deliberate turning away from Him and so does not wholly block the inflow of sanctifying grace. Mortal sins involve more serious actions and are committed with greater awareness of wrongdoing. (See Romans 3:23, 3:10, 8:38–39; James 2:10–11.)

How Can a Person Be Saved?

People must hear the gospel salvation message (Matthew 13:20, 24:14), get convicted by the good news of Jesus Christ (2 Chronicles 7:14; Acts 2:38), confess all known sins (1 John 1:9–10), repent (Acts 3:19), and accept Him as their Lord and Savior (John 1, 14).

Even those who consider themselves followers of Christ but are still committing sin must repent and forsake all to gain salvation. If you confess with your mouth, "Jesus is Lord," and believe in your heart that God raised Him from the dead, you will be saved (see Romans 10:9–10). For "everyone who calls on the name of the Lord will be saved" (Romans 10:13).

> For God so loved the world, that he gave his only Son, that whoever believes in him should not perish but have eternal life. (John 3:16)

Chapter 9

SALVATION

Salvation means "safe" or "saved" (Luke 1:71, 77; 19:9). It refers to deliverance of the soul from sin and its consequences (Philippians 2:12; Romans 1:16; 1 Thessalonians 5:8–9; Acts 15:6–11; 2 Thessalonians 2:13–15); forgiveness from transgression; liberation from immorality; reconciling with our heavenly Father, which comes as a ramification of penitence from wrongdoing (Matthew 24:12–13; Romans 10:1, 9; Matthew 1:21; Acts 4:12; Titus 2:11–14); and faith in our Lord and Savior Jesus's expiating sacrifices on the cross of martyrdom. Salvation is the foundational work of grace, which everyone must receive before becoming a Christian.

Without this experience through faith in Christ, the Christendom would not exist or be considered trustworthy. This original word of grace experience is the footing on which everyone can become a genuine Christian.

Simply put, God's plan for salvation is divine amorousness chronicled in the pages of the Holy Bible. Scriptural salvation is the Almighty's method of providing His children deliverance from darkness, sin, and spiritual death through repentance and faith in our Lord and Savior Jesus Christ.

According to the Old Testament in the tome of Exodus, the concept of salvation is entrenched in the promised land, Israel's deliverance from Egypt. At that time, the custom was that, whenever someone sinned, that person killed or sacrificed an animal, such as a cow or a goat, for the forgiveness of their sins. As for the New Testament, it reveals the source of salvation as our Lord Jesus Christ. By exercising faith in Him, believers are truly saved from God's verdict of sin and its consequence.

Then, we must question ourselves, *Why salvation?* According to the

Holy Bible, specifically in the beginning with the book of Genesis, Adam and Eve defied God and were immediately parted from God through sin. Our God is a holy God, and His holiness requires His followers to be holy by daily living holy and righteous lives. Failure on the part of folks who claim to be children of God requires that they face chastisement and recompense (atonement) for sin.

Moreover, only a flawless, faultless sacrifice, presented in just the right way, could pay for our sin. Jesus Christ, the only Son of God, was a flawless man of God who came to provide the pure, complete, and everlasting sacrifice to remove, atone, and make eternal recompense for sin. Why is this so? The omnipotent God, our Creator, cares and loves us so much that He desires an intimate relationship with us.

How Do We Receive Salvation?

The good news of repentance unto salvation in Christ is the only hope for humankind. People who ignore or refuse it will have their part in hell. In John 14:6; Jesus said, "I am the way, the truth, and the life: no man come unto the Father, but by me." Also, the apostle Peter emphasized the same truth in the scripture that says, "Neither is their salvation in any other: for there is no other name under heaven given among man, whereby we must be saved" (Acts 4:12).

Jesus Christ is the Author of our eternal salvation, which He acquired for us through His death on the cross (Acts 20:28b). We received salvation in Jesus Christ through repentance from our sins by faith. We are required to turn away from sinful behaviors and surrender all to God through faith, trusting in our Lord and Savior Jesus.

Christ will forgive us all our sins and set us on the path to life with the Lord. We cannot earn salvation or merit it. He freely gave it to us.

What Is the Path to Receive Salvation?

In order to obtain salvation, we must exercise faith in our Lord and Savior Jesus Christ and demonstrate that faith by being continually obedient to His instructions and spoken words (Acts 4:10, 12; Romans

10:9–10; Hebrews 5:9). The Bible illustrates that we must do works, or performances of obedience, to prove that our faith is active. However, according to James 2:24 and 26, this does not indicate that you can earn salvation. It is a gift from the Almighty God, based on His undeserved kindness and His grace, as stated in Ephesians 2:8–9.

Can a Believer Lose Out on Salvation?

The Bible reveals in the book of Hebrews 2:1, "Therefore, it is impossible to draft away!" It can happen sluggishly, bit by bit, by passively going with the flow of this current demonized era in which people disregard the will of God and allow their initial love for the Almighty to go cold. Similarly, Revelation 3:16 says, "So then, because you are lukewarm, and neither cold nor hot, I will vomit you out of my mouth."

It is evident that countless Christians have experienced friends' or relatives' leaving the church and, seemingly, the faith. For this reason, there is a misconception and controversy regarding whether those relatives and friends are saved forever and whether they will receive eternal life after death. The Holy Bible unveils answers about the inevitability of salvation and the negative effects of falling away from the faith.

For instance, Hebrews 6:4–8 is frequently construed as saying that Christians can lose their salvation, as the apostle Paul discusses the negative consequences of turning away from God. Another scripture that is regularly used to support this stance is 2 Timothy 1:18–20. It says that, when people habitually continue in iniquities and do not repent of them, they lose their salvation. Once the indwelling spirit departs from people, they are left on their own and are powerless.

Furthermore, many are deeply concerned about losing their salvation. They can lose out on salvation if they are complacent, careless Christians and if they don't take care. For example, it's just like being saved from drowning in a river: in one minute, the same person could fall or jump back into the river. What do you think would happen to this person?

Another scenario to clarify this concept involves a person who has been saved from habitual immoralities but who fails to keep exercising his faith and staying away from things that cause evil, which can lead to a pandemic sin. Committing iniquity could easily cause people to lose out on salvation.

For this reason, the Holy Bible implores Christians who have formally received salvation to be tenacious in maintaining the faith, as stated in Jude 3. It is imperative that those who have been saved heed the warning, "Keep working out your own salvation with fear and trembling" (Philippians 2:12).

So Will Everybody Be Saved?

In 2 Thessalonians 1:9 (KJV), the Bible says, "Who shall be punished with everlasting destruction from the presence of the Lord, and from the glory of His power." No! Not everyone will be saved in the end. Luke 13:23–24 (KJV) says, "Then said one unto Him, Lord, are there few that be saved? And He said unto them, strive to enter in at the strait gate: for many, I say unto you, will seek to enter in, and shall not be able." When our Lord and Savior Jesus was asked, He was emphatically bold and did not hide anything. Throughout the scripture, He taught us what to do to be saved. Most of us are still ignoring His teaching, and because of that, many are going astray.

Salvation from Sin

Salvation is the deliverance from the power of darkness and the consequences of sin. Romans 3:23–24 says, "For all have sinned and fall short of the glory of God, and all are justified freely by His grace through the redemption that came by Jesus Christ."

Assurance of Salvation

The followers of Christ may have assurance of their salvation through faith in Jesus Christ. Ephesians 2:8–9 reads, "For by grace are ye saved through faith; and that not of ourselves. It is the gift of God, through the work of the Holy Spirit."

Moreover, it is disheartening that record numbers of individuals in the Christendom haven't been able to enjoy and take advantage of the kind of lives they should be living as believers because they are not confident about the assurance of salvation. Regrettably, some strive to become saved by themselves, and because of the limited human strength to gain assurance of salvation, they continue to be dragged back into immoralities and their inability to live a Christlike life—fully, victoriously, and abundantly. In 1 John 5:4, we read, "For whatsoever is born of God overcometh the World: and this the victory that overcometh the world, even our faith."

For believer to have assurance of salvation, they must have a solid and assertive comprehension that their transgressions are pardoned. This assurance means that they are saved and are now members of God's family.

The main purpose of Jesus Christ's coming into this world and dying on the cross of Calvary was to save sinners, but a lot of His followers are in doubt about their salvation. Some wonder whether they will make it to heaven or not. People who are doubtful about the assurance of their salvation may find it difficult to be victorious over iniquity, the wisdom of the devil, temptation, persecution, and other challenges. Assurance of salvation is just like a travel document. If travelers don't have their documents with them, they cannot take the chance of traveling to other country.

In my own experience, some friends with whom I used to fellowship were habitually confessing their sins, whether a preacher made an altar call or not. They were confused and unsure of the assurance of their salvation.

I pondered this and realized that one of the reasons we are so confused or having difficulty believing is that we feel we can work this out by ourselves, but salvation is the work of grace through faith in Jesus Christ. Salvation is not tied to any human efforts. It is not earned by regularly going to church, being a church member, or giving alms.

Additionally, Christ died on the cross for this. Therefore, we must repent (John 1:12) and believe in Him. He is the only Son of God, and He came to earth in the form of man and died for our sins. He stayed in the grave for three days, rose again, and ascended to heaven to sit on the right side of God.

Our Lord and personal savior Jesus Christ requires all of His followers to repent of all known sins in order to be saved from them. In Mark 1:15, we read, "The time is fulfilled, and the kingdom of God is at hand, repent and believe in the gospel." Therefore, repentance and faith go together because, if you believe that Christ is the Lord and Savior who saves, which is faith in Jesus, you have a transformed mind about your sin and you forsake it.

Also, salvation is freedom from outward sins. As you have steadily come to accept Jesus Christ as your Lord and Savior, you have become saved by receiving your salvation and believing deeply in your heart that Jesus is the only Son of God in the universe, was born of the Virgin Mary, died for our sins on the cross of Calvary, rose from the dead after three days in the tomb and ascended into heaven, and now sits on the right side of God.

You can spiritually identify as a person who is saved through the following preparedness and spiritual actions:

- You must have heard the good news message of Jesus Christ (Mark 16:15; Romans 1:16; Luke 4:18; Isaiah 61:1; Mark 1:1, 14–15; Matthew 24:14).
- You must confess that Jesus Christ is the Son of God (1 John 4:15).
- You must obey and keep the commandments of God (1 John 5:3).
- You become upset when you realize that you have committed sin (1 John 3:9).
- You stay away from sin (1 John 5:18).
- You avoid idols (1 John 5:21).
- You get baptized, as Jesus Christ commanded.
- You tell others about your new faith in Jesus Christ.
- You make yourself available and spend time with the Lord. You set aside devotional time daily and develop the habit of reading the Holy Bible, memorizing Bible verses, and praying to Him sincerely. As you read His word, you present your supplication for the Lord to increase your faith and understanding of the Holy Bible.
- You have quiet time when you wake up in the early morning, depending on your spiritual strength. You read the Holy Bible, pray, and meditate on His words.

- You involve yourself in fellowship with other believers. You build a group of Christian affiliates to address questions you might have and to be your support system.
- You locate a local church where you can fellowship and worship the Lord incessantly.

Chapter 10

BELIEVERS' SANCTIFICATION

The apostles' abhorrence in 2 Corinthians 7:1 involves detailed or complete sanctification. It is essential that we purify ourselves from the entire filthiness of the flesh and spirit, perfecting sacredness in the fear of the Almighty.

The second work of grace after accepting salvation is sanctification (Hebrews 2:1–13). The Lord and Savior Jesus Christ is our sanctifier. Hebrews 13:12 says, "Wherefore Jesus also, that He might sanctify the people with His own blood, suffered without the gate." Here, we see that Jesus shed His precious blood to sanctify every saved individual to be pure as He is.

This sanctification experience, which is the second work of grace, truly transforms and makes people Christlike and united with Him in life, purpose, and service. It qualifies us to live forever with Him in the places prepared for us in heaven.

God is holy and can transform our lives to be holy as well. As believers, we must consecrate ourselves, hunger, and thirst (2 Timothy 2:21). We will be united in purity of heart (Hebrews 12:14).

Sanctification inspires Christians to set themselves apart from a worldly lifestyle and instead adhere to a godly lifestyle, from pleasure to a sacred purpose or religious use, to consecrate themselves and go from sin to redemption, holiness, and righteousness. I presume that the primary goal of every follower of Jesus Christ is to repent of all known sins and to obtain salvation, with the desire to continuously serve the Almighty until the end of time. It is not by our own power that we receive these works of grace and spiritual empowerment from the Lord, so it is imperative that we seek sanctification after gaining salvation.

Christians who are sanctified are believed to draw closer to the Lord Jesus Christ and to be more effective in their ministries. For instance, whether you would like to be a promise keeper, a missionary, an evangelist, or a worker in the vineyard of God, you must wholeheartedly seek the face of the Lord for sanctification.

Sanctification is amazingly effective in assisting Christians in setting themselves apart from things that cause sin and drawing believers intimately closer to the omnipotent God. Why is that so? Because, Christians who are sanctified are being empowered by the Holy Spirit; are bold in proclaiming and articulating God's word; are obedient to the Holy Spirit's redirection; will withstand hardship, persecution, and adversity; have the spiritual ability to overcome temptation; and are able to freely operate in the gifts of the Holy Spirit that clearly bring the true word of God to life.

Sanctification is also the method of procuring inviolability, of becoming holy. Holiness is a gift given by the awesome power of God to followers of Christ that transforms believers to set them apart for a particular use in an exceptional purpose of the work of God. Our God is pure and requires His servants or followers to be holy.

Sanctification is a spiritual gift that the Holy Ghost pours upon genuine born-again Christians to help them be effective in times of spiritual and physical challenges. It also brings followers of Christ closer to Him. Likewise, as a born-again Christian, you need sanctification to be equipped to transmit or carry out the vision and mission of God with ease.

The Holy Bible reiterates that the human heart is very wicked (Jeremiah 17:9–10) and quick to fall from the faith. Hence, sanctification, which is orchestrated by the Holy Spirit, will increase our faith and motivate us to live holy and righteous lives as we continue to serve.

In addition, sanctification is the awesome work of the Holy Spirit. Sincere born-again Christians are empowered by the Holy Spirit, setting themselves apart from sinful lives and ushering sinners into holy and blameless lives that are pleasing to God. Although the Bible indicates that no one is righteous (Romans 3:10–31), we must desire to live holy and righteous lives.

Furthermore, when we have gained salvation, it is not spiritually appropriate to stop there. The need to grow and spiritually mature is crucial for followers of Christ who would like to totally surrender unto the Lord. To be used for His purpose, believers must seek to be sanctified because sanctification draws them intimately nearer to the Lord and Savior Jesus Christ. Sanctified Christians are those who have been spiritually impacted with unwavering obedience by faith through Christ. Sanctification also prepares followers of Christ to practice living holy and righteous lives through their walk with the Lord. Additionally, sanctified believers must exhibit pure meditation and a pure heart, anointed and impacted with abundant love for Christ and His people.

At this pivotal point in your spiritual voyage, the Holy Spirit will empower you to overcome future trials, challenges, and temptations and encourage you to desire fruitfulness and to grow more spiritually and compassionately. As a sanctified Christian, you must be spiritually embedded in the word of God and willing to go the extra mile in helping the needy, ensuring that the gospel reaches all nations and is heard in and around the entire world (Matthew 28:18–20).

Beloved, God's purpose for your life and mine is for us to be sanctified. Sanctification ushers us into becoming like His perfect Son, Jesus Christ. This is a spiritual process and is not accomplished through our determination, resolve, strength, or power but by the Holy Spirit, as we completely yield or surrender our lives to His control and are filled with Him.

Moreover, sanctification theology is a gradual, preset-by-preset spiritual process through which believers are made holy through the action of the Holy Spirit.

As we deeply discuss Christians' setting themselves apart, gaining purity of mind, and living holy and righteous lives, the three main aspects of sanctification are as follows:

- Personal sanctification
- Progressive sanctification
- Ultimate sanctification

In personal sanctification, the Jesus Christ follower is in union with Him as a believer and has already been justified and declared righteous. In Romans 8:1–11, the apostle Paul describes how sanctification is worked out progressively throughout the life of the follower of Christ, who walks according to the spirit. Also, personal and ultimate sanctification are entirely the work of the Almighty God.

Progressive sanctification requires the cooperation of the Christian who was commanded to be filled with the Holy Spirit. Additionally, progressive sanctification is what gradually separates the children of the omnipotent God from the world and makes them more and more like Jesus Christ.

Sanctification is a process, beginning with justification and continuing throughout believers' lives. It is a three-stage process:

- past
- present
- future

The first stage occurs at the beginning of a person's Christian life. It is the preliminary moral transformation, a break from the power of the love of iniquity. It is the pivotal point at which we followers of Christ can count ourselves "dead to sin but alive to God" (Romans 6:11). Once sanctification has begun, we are no longer under sin's dominion (Romans 6:14). Believer, continue practicing with the desire of developing a loving righteousness. As the apostle Paul wrote, we are to become "slaves to righteousness" (Romans 6:17–18).

The second stage of sanctification takes a lifetime to complete. As followers of Christ grow in grace, they are progressively but steadily transforming to be more like Christ (2 Corinthians 3:18). This occurs in a process of daily spiritual renewal (Colossians 3:10). In Philippians 3:12 (KJV), the apostle Paul says, "Not as though I had already attained, either were already perfect: but I follow after, if that I may apprehend that for which also, I am apprehended of Christ Jesus." Here, we see that the apostle asserted that he had not reached perfection but that he "pressed on" to achieve everything Christ desired for him.

The third and last stage of sanctification occurs in the future. When followers of Christ die, their spirits go to be with Jesus (2 Corinthians 5:6–8). As believers, we are aware that nothing unclean can enter heaven (Revelation 21:27), so followers of Christ must be made perfect at that time.

The Almighty God's work in sanctification requires all three members of the Trinity. God the Father is continually at work in His children "to will and to work for His good pleasure" (Philippians 2:13). He transforms our desires, makes us want to please Him, and gives us the power to do so. Christ earned our sanctification on the cross of Calvary and, in essence, has become our sanctification (1 Corinthians 1:30) and the "perfecter of our faith" (Hebrews 12:2). The Holy Spirit is the primary agent of our sanctification (1 Corinthians 6:11; 2 Thessalonians 2:13; 1 Peter 1:2), and He produces in us the fruit of sanctification (Galatians 5:22–23).

Believers' role in sanctification is both passive and active. Passively, we are to trust the Almighty God to sanctify us, presenting our bodies to God (Romans 6:13; 12:1) and yielding to the Holy Spirit. Actively, we are responsible for choosing to do what is right. In 1 Thessalonians 4:4 (KJV), the Bible says, "That every one of you should know how to possess his vessel in sanctification an honor." This requires putting to death the "misdeeds of the body" (Romans 8:13), striving for holiness (Hebrews 12:14), fleeing immorality (1 Corinthians 6:18), cleansing ourselves from every defilement (2 Corinthians 7:1), and having faith (2 Peter 1:5–11).

Moreover, both the passive and active roles are essential for a healthy Christian life. In more detail, the passive role tends to lead to careless, spiritual laziness and a neglect of spiritual discipline. The result of this course of action is lack of spiritual maturity. The active role can lead to legalism, pride, and self-righteousness. The result of this is a joyless Christian life. It is imperative that we recollect that we pursue holiness, but only as God empowers us. The result is a consistent, mature Christian life that faithfully reflects the nature of God.

Positional sanctification occurs when believers are justified at salvation and declared righteous in conformity with the image of Jesus Christ (Romans 8:29). This salvation process is entirely orchestrated by the highest God, or the work of God.

Experiential sanctification is a postconversion experience of the church-age believer who enters into fellowship with God by confessing any known sin to the Father when necessary, followed by obedience to the Father's will, which is revealed by the Spirit through the word of God (1 John 1:9; 1 John 2:5).

Sanctification is experienced by Christ followers who submit to the desires of the Spirit, which constitutes being filled with the Holy Spirit as is commanded of Christians in Ephesians 5:18 (Romans 8:5–6). This obedience also constitutes obeying the command to let the word of Christ richly dwell in our souls (Colossians 3:16) and enables the Spirit to reproduce the character of Christ in believers (Galatians 5:22–23). Similarly, experiential sanctification is the process through which believers grow and mature in walking with the Lord Almighty and gain a lot of spiritual experience.

Thus, the objective here is Christlikeness, the ramifications of the ministry of the Holy Spirit in producing godliness in the life of Christ followers. In essence, progressive sanctification is becoming experienced in what believers already are positionally in Jesus Christ.

Moreover, the Holy Spirit operates in the following of Jesus Christ to free believers experientially from the power of immorality and death. Romans 12:2 says, "And do not be conformed to this world, but be transformed by the renewing of your mind, that you may prove what the will of God is, that which is good and acceptable and perfect."

The progress of sanctification, or becoming spiritually mature, is marked by conflict and spiritual warfare because believers' new lives in Christ are not in conformity with the world. They are rejected by Satan and fought by the sinful mature within humans. The presence of the Holy Spirit creates conflict and tension within humankind and the tricks of the devil aim to keep people unsafe in serving the Lord.

Ultimate sanctification is the Holy Spirit's effort to make followers of Christ holy. When the Holy Spirit creates faith in believers, He renews in them the image of the omnipotent God so that, by His power, Christ followers produce good works. These good works are not meritorious but show the faith in the Christians' hearts (Ephesians 2:8–10; James 2:18). The Bible says in 1 Thessalonians 5:23 (KJV), "And the very God of peace sanctify you wholly; and I pray God your whole spirit and soul and body be preserved blameless unto the coming of our Lord Jesus Christ." Therefore, it is the complete sanctification of the Christian's spirit, soul, and body being preserved blameless at the coming of our Lord Jesus Christ. Ultimate sanctification, sometimes referred to as glorification, is the final stage in the process of salvation (2 Peter 1:1–11).

Chapter 11

CONSECRATION

Consecration establishes the spiritual separation of born-again Christians from things that are unclean, especially anything that would pollute our association with the heavenly Father, who is perfect beyond all doubt. Consecration also carries the implied meaning of sanctification, holiness, or purification.

The importance of our being consecrated or becoming pure in our relationship with God is highlighted in an event that occurs in the Bible, in the Old Testament book of Joshua. We see that, after more than thirty-nine years in the wilderness, the Israelites are about to voyage across the Jordan River and into the promised land. Joshua commands the people of Israel to sanctify (Joshua 3:5) or consecrate themselves, for the next day the Lord will do miracles among them. The Bible reveals also in 1 Corinthians 7:1–6 that the children of Israel are commanded to cleanse and change their garments, and the married couples are to dedicate themselves wholly to the Lord.

Likewise, consecration is the our absolute relinquishment to our heavenly Father. Consecration entails spiritual discipline, a well-organized planning of spiritual errands, and an unwavering faith through Jesus Christ in our daily Christian walk. It also means exhibiting an indwelling spiritual zeal, or the Holy Ghost, that is embedded in us as born-again Christians and that enables us or gives us consistent strength and strategies to continue this valuable and endless spiritual journey until the coming of Christ.

As born-again Christians, consecration involves our lives being a sacrifice to Jesus Christ, meaning that we are totally separated from the defilement of the worldly lifestyle. Daily, we must live out our lives as a "holy" and "royal" (1 Peter 2:9–10) priesthood for the glory of God. Romans 12:1 (KJV) says, "I beseech you therefore, brethren, by the mercies of God, that ye present your bodies a living sacrifice, holy, acceptable unto God, which is your reasonable service."

In the passage, the apostle Paul is encouraging us to present our bodies as living sacrifices, holy, well-pleasing to the Almighty God as our reasonable service. When we offer ourselves to the Lord, we no longer belong to ourselves but to the Almighty God.

For instance, the conversion of a newcomer is a thrilling and joyous occasion, and the Christian family recognizes it as the inception of a new birth, or a new life in Christ. Converts desire to live a Christlike life, and it is a lifelong journey; it does not end with the conversion. They instantaneously crave more intimacy. Hence, this is when they have the greatest spiritual opportunity to explore His word by praying without ceasing, searching the scriptures daily, and seeking the face of our Lord and personal savior for more knowledge and understanding of His word.

Followers of Christ have wholeheartedly surrendered their lives into the awesome hands of our Lord and Savior, and for them, being saved and born again, with the Holy Spirit indwelling in them, and living a Christlike life is spiritually rewarding and thrilling. But this is just the beginning of a lifelong spiritual journey. Just as new souls in Christ grow spiritually, the mature and well-equipped Christians can handle spiritual issues and withstand the tricks of the devil, guided by the spiritual power of the omnipotent God. We believers endeavor to proceed onward, stage by stage, in this spiritual process.

Subsequently, when we are renewed, it is of paramount importance that the succeeding process in our lifelong spiritual journey be one of complete submission, or giving of ourselves to the Lord and allowing Him to use us for His purpose.

Moreover, consecration is also used in the official ordination of people to be deacons, preachers, bishops, or missionaries. The unique spiritual title usually refers to special, spirit-filled individuals who have completely dedicated their lives to serving our Lord and Savior, with zero transgressions. Because consecration itself is the foundation of spiritual experience, we willingly give or surrender ourselves to the omnipotent God as a living sacrifice.

Chapter 12

DEDICATION TO SERVICE

Dedication to service is a state of being committed to God's work as well as a ceremony for the induction of a promise keeper, a child's birth, and other significant events. Dedication is the feeling of being a born-again Christian. Colossians 3:23–24 says, "Whatever you do, work heartily, as for the Lord and not for men, knowing that from the Lord you will receive the inheritance as your reward. You are serving the Lord Christ."

Christians who are dedicated to the work of God persistently and consistently do the will of God through faith in Jesus Christ. They are believers who are spiritually filled and are organized in planning their own lives and church programs. They are straightly and spiritually self-controlled, dependable, committed to uninterrupted prayer time, and able to set spiritual goals and meet the deadlines. Believers dedicated to service assist the followers of Christ in starting strong and prepare for known and unknown trials and temptations that arise in the lives of Christians.

Such spiritual leaders are prayerful people ready to overcome many issues that may come to hinder their progress, no matter how difficult that task of reaching out to the lost souls and preaching the word of God may be. For instance, we all are aware that hard work and dedication are the path to success, but the way is not always simple. This isn't new to us and is just part of life, but the scripture is provided to guide and inspire us during even the harshest of times. Our heavenly Father wants us to prosper in all aspects of our lives, and He gave us the power to do just that.

If you are spiritually determined (James 1:12; 1 Corinthians 16:13) and have willingly made up your mind to carry out God's vision for the church, you will always be motivated and yearn to see the reasons to continue performing what you are doing faithfully through Christ. People who are embodied within this work of grace through in Jesus Christ are clear that they are being directed and guided by the Holy Ghost. Their daily strength (Habakkuk 3:19; Isaiah 40:29) to perform these tasks is from the Lord.

Dedicated servants in the vineyard of the Lord God are obviously believed to be dead to immorality. Their meditation and focus are always on kingdom-building, evangelism, outreach, feeding the poor, prison ministry, soul-winning, and mission vision. Also, they are usually considered to be indispensable leaders and always available to give counsel to incoming new members and the church.

Chapter 13

WHY IS IT IMPORTANT TO BE A BORN-AGAIN CHRISTIAN?

It is important to be a born-again Christian because our Lord told us in the book of John that only those who are born again can enter the kingdom of God, while those who are not born again cannot. The term *born-again Christian* applies to individuals who have already heard the gospel message, gotten convicted, acknowledged that they are sinners and need a savior, repented from all known sins, accepted Jesus as their Lord, and believed that He is the only Son of God who came and died on the cross for our sins. He was buried in the grave, and after three days, He arose and ascended to heaven, where He sits at the right hand of God.

Moreover, when we answer God's offer of mercy and eternal life through our Lord and Savior Jesus Christ, confess our sins, and invite Him into our lives to be our Savior, Jesus Christ comes into our hearts. And when His Holy Spirit truly comes in and fills us and transforms us, we are genuinely born again and saved.

Furthermore, Jesus Christ perceived the significance and the indispensability of being born-again Christians, as without it no one can enter the heavenly kingdom of God. He emphasizes this in John 3, verses 3 and 5 (KJV): "Jesus answered and said unto him, "Verily, verily, I say unto thee, except a man be born again, he cannot see the kingdom of God.... Jesus answered, Verily, verily, I say unto thee, except a man be born of water and of the Spirit, he cannot enter the kingdom of God."

According to these verses, we must be genuinely born of water and of the Spirit, or else we cannot enter the kingdom of God. Does this caution connect to the rapture and the Holy Spirit being taken away from earth? If that is the case, will those "ordinary" Christians who have not been born again be left behind and unable to be taken in the rapture?

Additionally, since the Lord clearly said we cannot enter the kingdom of God unless we are born again, it is reasonable to conclude that only born-again believers will be raptured. Being born of water refers to the physical, which is the first birth, and being born of the Spirit is spiritual, which is the second birth. All of this occurs when we declare our belief that the Lord Jesus Christ died for our sins and that we accept him as our Lord and Savior because, without His intervention on our behalf, we would not have the power to reconcile with our Creator.

The significance of being genuinely born again is that a great reward awaits those who are. Why not repent of all known sins and renew your mind to avoid being left behind? "So then, what will it profit us to gain everything in the world and lose our souls?" (Matthew 16:26; Mark 8:36). Just sit for a while and meditate upon how important it is to make up your mind and repent of any known sins and allow Jesus to take control of your life.

The word of God says, "Whoever believes on Him will not be put to shame." For there is no distinction between Jew and Greek; the same Lord overall will reach out to all who call upon Him. "Whoever calls on the name of the Lord shall be saved" (Romans 10:13).

Thus, if people realize that they are sinners, get convicted, invite Christ into their hearts, repent, confess with their mouths that the Lord Jesus Christ is the one and only Savior, and believe honestly in their hearts that the Almighty God has raised Him from the dead, they are saved. With the heart, a person believes unto righteousness, and with the mouth, confession is made unto salvation.

Likewise, Jesus Christ told the truth that "no Christian can see the kingdom of God, unless that Christian be born again" (John 3:3). Consequently, Christians are born again to prepare themselves for heaven.

So many of us claim to be Christians in this world or on earth, striving with the ambition of going to heaven. But the reality is that we need to be possessed by the Almighty God, which is to be born again. When Christians are born again, there arises a dynamic and radical change within them, which includes spiritual sensitivity, a total dependence on the Lord for everything, and total abhorrence for sin.

Besides your love and yearning for Jesus and others, you are different from the way you served God before and the love you had for God's people. Family members, people in your neighborhood, and your church members will soon begin to perceive the zeal of service and love for others in you. This newly born-again Christian will be on spiritual fire, spreading the gospel, consistently praying and interceding for others, organizing small groups and a prison ministry, visiting sick patients in hospitals, sharing testimonies of God's goodness, and preaching the good news about Christ to immediate family members, neighbors, friends, and anyone else.

Most importantly, you will have become a spiritual vessel embodied by the Holy Ghost, receiving power and direction from above. You will be mature in performing spiritual duties in the vineyard of the highest living God of heaven.

Chapter 14

EVIDENCE OF A BORN-AGAIN CHRISTIAN

Our Lord and personal savior Jesus Christ said,

> Not everyone who said unto me, Lord, Lord, shall enter God's kingdom of heaven; but he that doeth the will of my Father, which is in heaven. Many will say to me in that day, Lord, Lord, have we not prophesied in thy name? And in thy name have cast out devils? And in thy name done wonderful works? And then will I profess unto them, I never knew you: depart from me, ye that work iniquity. (Matthew 7:21–23)

As we perceive in these verses, Jesus Christ did not deny that a few ill-advised souls have false hope of gaining entry into His dwelling place. He declares that many do. Christ chat to the believer and those professed Christians who believe that they are being born-again followers of Christ. In today's world, many misguided professed Christians think that they will find it easy to enter the kingdom of God. These are people who may think that they are saved Christians and are going to heaven based on lip service but are still walking in darkness and confidentially committing immorality.

Nevertheless, when the day of acknowledgment comes, at which time they will stand before the judgment throne of God, they will be denied, much to their surprise. Remember, Jesus Christ said he will tell them, "Depart from me, I know you not."

Moreover, once people become born-again Christians, they will immediately begin to perceive and experience changes in their lives that are unexplainable in the natural sense. In this new and exciting spiritual experience, believers do not forfeit who they are but become better people in Christ, have new spiritual strength, and practice thinking above that of other Christians who are not yet born again. They begin to see themselves with an unusual motivating zeal, have feelings of wanting to read and study the Holy Bible continuously, pray for themselves and intercede for others, and feel a boldness in teaching and preaching the word of God to others. They will seek to win as many lost souls as possible and, having these souls won, will be established in the saving knowledge of God. Such people are no longer normal and complicit Christians but always zealous about the world of God and on fire for Jesus.

Therefore, effectual and genuine born-again Christians might want to review these helpful points that bring radical transformations:

- You will perceive positive changes in your spiritual life and increase in your love for the Lord and empathy for others.
- You will still experience impediments and persecutions in life, but you will be fully dependent on God, and because of that you will handle them spiritually better and know that God is working in your life.
- You will have a genuine longing to be pleasing to the Almighty God and live in obedience to Him and His word.
- In countless instances, broken relationships and marriages may be reinstated or restored.
- You may be driven to do things you have always wanted to do but believed you were not moral enough or deserving enough to pursue.
- You will have a burning longing to serve God and share His love and the gospel with the world and with people who haven't heard the good news.
- You will have an appetite for more of God's word. This appetite will result in more interest in studying God's word, the Holy Bible,

and seeking God's will in your life. The more you get to intimately know God, the closer you will become to Him.
- You will be bold in proclaiming God's word.

The Peace by Jesus website (http://www.peacebyjesus.witnesstoday.org) listed some evidence of what a genuine born-again Christian is, shared here for our learning:

Regeneration (Titus 3:5; Ezekiel 36:26; John 3:5; 1 John 3:9; 1 Peter 1:23; John 3:1–36): There comes a time in people's lives when they understand their immoral situation, and with utterly no expectation of salvation via their endeavors or virtues, they realize that they are sinners; repent of their immoral situations; confess their sins; believe (1 John 5:1; 2 Corinthians 5:17); accept Jesus Christ, who came and died for their sins; know that He was buried and, after three days in the grave, rose again as their Lord and Savior; and relinquish all unto Him.

Titus 3:5 says, "Not by works of righteousness which we have done, but according to His mercy He saved us, by the washing of regeneration, and renewing of the Holy Ghost." Acts 20:21 says, "Testifying both to the Jews, and also to the Greeks, repentance toward God, and faith toward our Lord Jesus Christ."

Water Baptism (1 Peter 3:21; Acts 2:38; Acts 22:16; Mark 16:16; 1 Corinthians 12:13; Matthew 3:11; Matthew 28:18–20): You were baptized as Christ commanded that you must be baptized through immersion in water. Acts 2:38 says, "Then Peter said unto them, Repent, and be baptized everyone of you in the name of Jesus Christ for the remission of sins, and ye receive the gift of the Holy Ghost." Acts 8:12 reads, "But when they believed Philip preaching the things concerning the kingdom of God, and the name of Jesus Christ, they were baptized, both men and women." Acts 2:40 states, "Then they that gladly received His word were baptized." In Acts 8:36–38, we read, "And as they went on their way, they came unto certain water: and the eunuch said, see, here is water; what doth hinder me to be baptized? And Philip said, if thou believe with all thy heart, thou mayest. And he answered and said, Jesus Christ is the son of God. And he commanded the chariot to stand still: and they went down into the water, both Philip and the eunuch; and he baptized him."

Experiencing Spiritual Jubilation (Habakkuk 3:17–18): At this point, you realize unusual new joy in Jesus Christ; you understand that the risen Christ was real and alive; and you also believe that your sins were forgiven and that you have been accepted into the family of God. Now you have experienced the actualities of being a spiritually born-again Christian. You have had the renewal of the heart, with new affections—a heartfelt, continuous yearning to understand the will of God according to the Holy Bible, receiving the power to consistently pray, and a distinctive soulful affection for other believers.

Acts 8:39 says, "When they were come up out of the water, the spirit of the Lord caught away Philip, that the eunuch saw him no more: and he went on his way, rejoicing." In 1 Corinthians 5:17, the Bible says, "Therefore if any man be in Christ, he is a new creature; old things are passed away, behold, all things are become new." We read in 1 Thessalonians 1:5–6, "For our gospel came not only unto word only, but also in power, and the Holy Ghost, and in much assurance as ye know what manner of men we were among you for your sake. And ye became followers of us, and of the Lord, having received the word in much affliction, with joy of the Holy Ghost."

Fellowship with Believers (Psalm 55:14; 1 John 1:7; Acts 2:42; 1 John 1:3): As you have repented from your sin to fully serve the Almighty, the God of the universe, our Creator, and the living and true God, you must continuously pursue Him and carefully follow His footsteps. Also, you must obey His unblemished words, which is the Holy Bible. You must consistently make yourself available to serve to affiliate and align yourself with believers, who will have a significant impact on you through your journey.

Acts 2:41 says, "Then they that gladly received his word were baptized: and the same day there were added unto them about three thousand souls." Acts 2:42 adds, "And they continued steadfastly in the apostles' doctrine and fellowship, and in the breaking of bread, and in prayers." In 1 Thessalonians 1:9, we read, "For they themselves show of us what manner of entering in we had unto you, and how ye turned to God idols to serve the living and true God."

Unshakable Prayer Life

As a born-again Christian, the onus is on you to pray directly to the omnipotent God and no other gods. You must pray in accordance with His word. As you increase your prayer life, you'll perceive the Almighty God spiritually motivating you to intercede for specific things or individuals and instantaneously answering your prayers.

Psalm 62:5–8 says,

> My soul, wait thou only upon God; for my expectation is from Him. He only is my rock and my salvation: He is my defense; I shall not be moved. In God is my salvation and my glory: the rock of my strength, and my refuge, is in God. Trust in him always; ye people, pour out your heart before Him: God is a refuge for us, Selah.

Acts 4:12 says, "Neither is their salvation in any other: for there is no other name under the heaven given among men, whereby we must be saved." In 1 Timothy 2:5, we read, "For there is one God, and one mediator between God and men, the man Christ Jesus." Hebrews 4:14–16 adds,

> Seeing then that we have a great high priest, that is passed into the heavens, Jesus the Son of God, let us hold fast our profession. For we have not a high priest which cannot be touched with the feeling of our infirmities; but was in all points tempted like as we are, yet without sin. Let us therefore come boldly unto the throne of grace, that we may obtain mercy, and find grace to help in time of need.

Revelation 8:4 states, "And the smoke of the incense, which came with the prayers of the saints, ascended up before God out of the angel's hand." John 14:14 says, "If ye shall ask anything in My name, I will do it." Also,

1 John 5:14 adds, "And this is the confidence that we have in Him, that, if we ask anything according to His will, He heareth us."

Adore Him

It is vital that you want to perceive the Lord Almighty, alone to be exalted, and to worship and praise Him. We should not be ashamed of adoration and honor, or of admiring and worshipping our Lord, because of His work of redemption. When I count my blessings and consider where and how He brought me through, I cannot afford to *not* praise my Lord and Savior Jesus Christ.

Psalm 21:13 says, "Be thou exalted, Lord, in thine own strength: So, will we sing and praise thy power." In 2 Thessalonians 1:12, we read, "That the name of our Lord Jesus Christ may be glorified in you, and ye in Him, according to the grace of our God and the Lord Jesus Christ." Philippians 1:20 says, "According to my earnest expectation and my hope, that in nothing I shall be ashamed, but that with all boldness, as always, so now also Christ shall be magnified in my body, whether it be by life, or by death." Then, 1 Peter 3:15 says, "But sanctify the Lord God in your hearts: and be ready always to give an answer to every man that asked you a reason of the hope that is in you with meekness and fear."

Evangelism

Craving for the lost souls, seeking their salvation by prayer, and sharing the word with them are spiritually significant in the lives of evangelists and church members. Acts 8:4 says, "Therefore they that were scattered abroad went everywhere preaching the word." In 1 Thessalonians 1:8, we read, "For from you sounded out the word of the Lord not only in Macedonia and Achaia, but also in every place your faith to God-ward is spread abroad; so that we need not to speak anything."

Since the day of John the Baptist, when he pleaded to the people to repent and be baptized, the Holy Bible intimately connects baptism with believing the good news, the gospel of salvation through Jesus Christ of Nazareth. "Jesus said to them, 'Go into all the world and preach the good news to all creation. Whoever believed and baptized will be saved, but whoever does not believe will be condemned."

According to the scriptures, specifically the book of Acts, when people are convicted, they must repent and be baptized in the name of Jesus Christ for the forgiveness of their sins (Acts 2:38).

Baptism signifies the washing away of one's sins. And it symbolizes the absolute truth or fact that, just as Jesus Christ died for your sins and mine, He was buried and rose again to life after three days in the grave.

Hence, when participating in baptism as Jesus commanded, we die to our sins and are buried with Christ by emulsion into the river, beneath the water in baptism, and we rise again to live a new life in Jesus Christ of Nazareth. "And now why are you waiting? Arise and be baptized, wash away your sins, calling on the name of our Lord and savior" (Acts 22:16).

Chapter 15

BENEFITS OF BEING A BORN-AGAIN CHRISTIAN

Most of the time, the burden that professionals face when seeking a job is determining what the benefit of that job will be. They may think, *If I accept this job, what will be my benefit?* or *How will I benefit from this company?* Job benefits are important for job seekers, so they make sure to research each company's profile before accepting a position.

In some instances, the benefits are valued higher than the salary. Thus, for a person yearning to be born again, his! Our eyes must always be on the possibility of being saved and the privileges of seeing our Lord and Savior Jesus Christ so that were are able to enter the kingdom of heaven. "What will it profit a person to gain the entire world and lose his soul?" (Mark 8:36; Matthew 16:16). There are countless benefits to being a born-again Christian, but some people are uninformed.

"As a servant of God, greater is he that is in you than he that is in the world" (1 John 4:4). The Holy Spirit is within us, and because of that we are protected. He is the one we depend on. He is our protector, provider, and guide, and He is with us in time of need, trouble, and prosecution. Most of all, it is because of Him that we have overcome. Can you imagine reclining in bed, sleeping like we are dead and not knowing anything that is happening around us but waking up in our right minds? Wow!

Moreover, there is a lot of dirt, particles, and pollution in the atmosphere and in our environment, but we breathe clean air. How is this possible? This was made possible for our benefit. Why not surrender all to follow Jesus and enjoy more?

If we can enjoy these and many other benefits on earth, don't you think there is more in heaven than what we have here in this wicked world? Why not repent and accept Jesus Christ as Lord so as not to miss the countless benefits in heaven?

Also, there are countless benefits to being a born-again Christian—benefits that never end, that we could never purchase with physical silver or gold. They are priceless, and if we continue being obedient to the word of God, vehemently refusing and avoiding immorality, consistently trusting in the Lord, and remaining dependent on Him, we are bound to enjoy all the benefits He has reserved for us.

The ultimate advantage is not just to secure a place in heaven forever, but while we are still on earth, He gives us the power to be justified by faith (Romans 5:1–2), meaning that the Lord made us innocent in the eyes of the Almighty God. We are declared free from the power of sin. We are being protected by the supernatural power of the Holy Spirit. So we have hope and victory over the enemy and a better understanding of God's word.

Ordinarily, it is okay for new converts to be confused and uncertain about salvation as they try to figure out whether their salvation is genuine. Nevertheless, it is imperative that we not be burdened by our longing for true salvation.

Once you have heard the gospel or the good news of Christ, invite Him into your life and accept Jesus as Lord and Savior, acknowledge that you are a sinner, and repent of any known sin. Now, you are filled with bursting assurance that Jesus Christ has come into your life (John 14:20). He has forgiven your sins (Colossians 2:13–14), and through Christ you have everlasting life (1 John 5:13).

We Relish God's Abundant Love (Psalms 36:7–9; Exodus 34:6; John 10:10)

Those yearning to be born again will receive spiritual power imparted internally by the Holy Ghost, who will be their best friend and helper in times of confusion, when needing strength to pray, and during decision-making. The Holy Spirit will protect you and speak to you in times of diverse challenges in life as you commit yourself to depend on Him.

Most importantly, allow yourself to surrender to the Holy Spirit as you proceed on this prolonged journey in walking with the Lord. The Holy Ghost will always be there to tutor you in every spiritual thing you need to know, as well as to teach you the scriptures as you persistently read the Holy Bible. Your daily helper, who is the Holy Spirit, will continue to empower you as you prepare presentations to train others, preach the gospel to congregations, do missionary work, and talk to others about God's word.

Being born-again Christians moves our lives in a positive direction and gives us the spiritual green light of assurance that we will be delivered from debauchery and its penalties, which did us no good but drew us into eternal condemnation and death.

As a genuine, born-again Christian, you have become part of God's household and have the right to perceive and to be escorted into the kingdom of God to live there jubilantly and eternally. This exceptional approach can be utilized only through spiritually exhibiting unshakable faith in Jesus Christ, our Lord and Savior.

Please recollect that it is imperative to admit and accept the fact that we are all sinners, and because of that we cannot satisfy the omnipotent God. Therefore, we need assistance to have a perfect affiliation with the Lord. We must also acknowledge and comprehend that Jesus Christ died in our place, fully paid for our sins, and made it conceivable for us (flawed humans) to interact with a flawless heavenly Father (God) and that our new affiliation with Him is completely dependent on the finished work of Jesus Christ at the cross of Calvary.

He did it on our behalf and not because of our virtuous deeds.

Bless with a New Life and Spiritual Empowerment (2 Corinthians 5:17; Ezekiel 36:26; Romans 1:2; Galatians 6:15)

Beloved, becoming a born-again Christian is an especially important spiritual step in drawing us intimately closer to the Almighty God, and there are so many uncountable physical and spiritual benefits that make one realize how delightful it is to be an obedient servant. If you consistently, and continuously obey the word of God, and remain in the realm of the Holy Spirit, without deviating from His word, the Lord will anoint you and protect you, from any weapon discovered against you. It shall not prosper.

In the book of Romans, the Bible specifies, "Being justified by faith we have peace with God through our Lord Jesus Christ. We also have access, by faith, to His grace, wherein we stand and rejoice in hope of the glory of God. And not so, but we glory in tribulations as well, knowing that tribulation worked patience" (Romans 5:1–3). This indwelling spirit (Holy Spirit) is available to assist us in overcoming temptations that come our way while we are serving the Lord. It will make us bold and give us power over the devil. When we speak and command the devil, he hears and obeys the command. The Holy Spirit will also enable us to be prayerful, get baptized in the Holy Ghost, be spiritually sensitive, receive deliverance from the power of darkness, make us bold in winning souls, and keep us joyful in times of trials and prosecution.

Though we were born in sin (Romans 3:20–23), we are justified by Jesus Christ. He is the one and only who can justify us. Therefore, justification can be rendered only by one who is just. A born-again Christian is a believer filled with the anointing of the Holy Ghost, bold in presenting the good news of Jesus Christ to converts, powerful in praying for others, delivered from darkness, and living a Christlike life.

It is critical that you acknowledge that you are a sinner, invite Christ into your life, repent of any known sin, and accept Him as Lord and Savior. At this point, your mind is renewed with the new life in Christ. As such, you are a new creation, just like a newborn baby straight from its mother's womb, eager to grow and begin going through the necessary baby steps to learn more about the new life in Christ. Beloved, you have just started a long and continuous Christian journey and spiritual relationship with the Lord that might last for life (2 Corinthians 5:17; Colossians 2:6–7).

Jubilating in the Power of Effectual Fervent Prayers (James 5:16; 1 Corinthians 2:9; Psalm 145:18; 1 Thessalonians 5:16–18; Philippians 4:6–7; Colossians 4:2; Mark 11:24; Jeremiah 29:12)

Most unbelievers do not really believe that it is possible for anyone who has accepted Jesus Christ as Lord and Savior to talk to Him. As a believer, you have the privilege to speak to your heavenly Father at any time you wish, through prayers, because prayer is communication with God. He hears and answers every word of prayer a believer prays. What can prayer *not* do? Jesus answers prayers (1 John 5:14–15; Mark 11:24).

It is also rewarding to acknowledge and comprehend that you can dialogue with your heavenly Father on any issue concerning yourself, family, souls, fellow believers, all nations, and more. There is nothing too minute or inconsequential to talk about with the Lord (Philippians 4:6).

Study Your Bible and Search the Scriptures Daily (2 Timothy 1:7, 2:15; Colossians 3:17; Hebrews 4:12; Joshua 1:8; Psalm 119:105; Revelation 1:3)

Diving deeper into the Bible by reading it and memorizing Bible verses daily helps you understand and benefit from the word of God. Every day as we search the scriptures, we see that it increases our faith and makes us dependent upon the Lord. The gospel is for our learning (2 Timothy 3:16) and our correction and to rebuke us to live according to the word.

Conclusion

Becoming a Christian is a great spiritual decision that moves you in a unique direction and allows Christ to dwell in you and transform your life. Accepting Jesus Christ as Lord and Savior makes you a follower of Christ, a believer or a Christian. But that is just the beginning; you must continuously long for increased faith in Jesus and unwaveringly proceed through the spiritual process by recognizing the fact that you are a sinner, confessing, inviting Jesus into your heart, accepting Him as your Lord and savior, stopping the things that cause you to sin, and sinning no more! Go through beginner and baptism classes; gain your salvation and sanctification; consecrate yourself; and love God, fellow believers, and others. Once you are continuously reliant on God, doing His will and obedient, you are considered a born-again Christian. As such, you do not do or encourage acts that will lead to sin because the Almighty God with whom you have reconciled through Christ does not like or condone sin.

How many Christians today can you point to and say, "This believer or these brethren are genuinely born again"? People who are born-again Christians can be identified by the kind of spirit they possess, which includes a godliness, positive attitude, a certain way of conducting themselves, integrity, living a Christlike life, caring for others, having an intimate relationship with Christ, being obedient to the word of God, teaching others what they have learned and motivating them to surrender their lives to Christ, and continuously serving the Lord until the end of time.

Jesus Christ is the way, the truth, and the life (John 14:6). He's the way to another life after this one, which is eternal life. Why would we endeavor to lose these important opportunities that are freely given to us and end up in hellfire and forever in condemnation? We can joyfully join Jesus in the many missions He promised if we first follow a few steps, which include acknowledging that we are sinners, inviting Him into our lives, accepting Him as Lord and Savior, repenting from any known sin, believing that Christ is the only Son of God who came and died on the cross of Calvary for the sins of humanity, and wholeheartedly serving Him. He is our Lord and Savior.

Printed in the United States
by Baker & Taylor Publisher Services